How to Inhabit the Earth

Bruno Latour

How to Inhabit the Earth

Interviews with Nicolas Truong

With the collaboration of Rose Vidal

Translated by Julie Rose

polity

Originally published in French as *Comment habiter la terre. Entretiens avec Nicolas Truong* © Les Liens qui Libèrent & Arte Éditions, 2022. This edition is published by arrangement with Les Liens qui Libèrent and Arte Éditions in conjunction with its duly appointed agents Books And More Agency #BAM, France. All rights reserved.

This English edition © Polity Press, 2024

Cet ouvrage a bénéficié du soutien du Programme d'aide à la publication de l'Institut français / This book is supported by the Institut français as part of the 'Programme d'aide à la publication'.

Polity Press
65 Bridge Street
Cambridge CB2 1UR, UK

Polity Press
111 River Street
Hoboken, NJ 07030, USA

ISBN-13: 978-1-5095-5946-6 (hardback)
ISBN-13: 978-1-5095-5947-3 (paperback)

A catalogue record for this book is available from the British Library.

Library of Congress Control Number: 2023934718

Typeset in 11/14 Sabon by Cheshire Typesetting Ltd, Cuddington, Cheshire
Printed and bound in Great Britain by CPI Group (UK) Ltd, Croydon

The publisher has used its best endeavours to ensure that the URLs for external websites referred to in this book are correct and active at the time of going to press. However, the publisher has no responsibility for the websites and can make no guarantee that a site will remain live or that the content is or will remain appropriate.

Every effort has been made to trace all copyright holders, but if any have been overlooked the publisher will be pleased to include any necessary credits in any subsequent reprint or edition.

For further information on Polity, visit our website:
politybooks.com

Contents

Introduction

Nicolas Truong

Wanting to pass on, to explain. To explain himself, as well, meaning to explain how coherent his thought actually was, a fact that had partly been masked by its apparently wide-ranging nature and the variety of subjects he tackled. In his Paris apartment, Bruno Latour threw himself into this series of interviews with a simplicity, an exuberance, and a force that only comes to the fore in moments when you know that life, and notably the life of the mind, is being cut short. There was a deep calm linked to a sense of urgency, an immanence indissociable from imminence, and the need to bring everything together, to sum it up, get it out there. A concern for clarity, a pleasure in conversation, that performance art. As if everything was becoming clearer as the end drew near. Bruno Latour died on 9 October 2022 at the age of seventy-five. He is one of the most important French intellectuals of his generation. 'France's most famous and misunderstood philosopher,' wrote the *New York Times* on 25 October 2018.

Introduction

A celebrity and celebrated abroad, recipient of the Holberg Prize (2013) and the Kyoto Prize (2021) for his whole body of work, Bruno was, indeed, misunderstood for a time in France, so disparate did his objects of study seem. It must be said that he delved into almost all realms of knowledge: ecology, the law, modernity, religion, and, of course, the sciences and technologies with his inaugural and explosive studies of laboratory life.

Bruno was all the more misunderstood as, with the notable exception of Michel Serres, with whom he conducted a round of interviews, *Eclaircissements*,[1] philosophy in France has often steered clear of the theory and practice of the sciences.

'He was the first to feel that the whole challenge for politics lay in the issue of ecology,' recalls sociologist Bruno Karsenti, as was attested, as early as 1999, by the publication of *Politiques de la nature*,[2] written in consonance with Serres's *Le contrat naturel* (1990).[3]

An iconoclastic sociologist

But without a doubt it was two books dedicated to ecology, and delivered in the form of questions, *Où atterir?* (Where do we land?)[4] and *Où suis-je?* (Where

---

[1] Published by François Bourin in 1992; reissued by Le Pommier in 2022. Published in English as *Conversations on Science, Culture and Time: Michel Serres with Bruno Latour* (University of Michigan Press, 1995); translated by Roxanne Lapidus.

[2] Published by La Découverte. Published in English as *Politics of Nature* (Harvard University Press, 2004); translated by Catherine Porter.

[3] Published in English as *The Natural Contract* (University of Michigan Press, 1995); translated by Elizabeth MacArthur and William Paulson.

[4] Published by La Découverte in 2017. Published in English as *Down to Earth* (Polity, 2018); translated by Catherine Porter.

am I?),[5] that brought this iconoclastic sociologist to a much broader public.

Born on 22 June 1947 in Beaune (Côte-d'Or) into a large bourgeois family of wine merchants, Bruno Latour grew to become one of the most influential philosophers of our time, inspiring a new generation of intellectuals, artists, and activists anxious to do something about the ecological disaster.

Ever since 'the intrusion of Gaia', in the words of the philosopher Isabelle Stengers,[6] with whom he enjoyed an enduring intellectual friendship, one chronicled by Philippe Pignarre in *Latour–Stengers, un double vol enchevetré*,[7] Bruno never stopped thinking about the 'new climate regime' we live in.[8] For 'we have changed worlds', he explained, since we entered the Anthropocene Age, in which man becomes a geological force. 'We're not living on the same Earth,' he maintained.[9]

From the 17th century on, the Moderns believed that the separation between nature and culture, between objects and subjects, was real. They contended that 'non-humans' were things that were alien to us, even though they never stopped engaging with them. This

---

[5] Published by La Découverte in 2021. Published in English as *After Lockdown: A Metamorphosis* (Polity, 2021); translated by Julie Rose.

[6] Isabelle Stengers, *Au Temps des catastrophes* (La Découverte, 2009), Published in English as *In Catastrophic Times: Resisting the Looming Barbarism* (Open Humanities Press, 2015; translated by Andrew Goffey.

[7] Published by Les Empêcheurs de penser en rond in 2021. Published in English as *Latour–Stengers: An Engtangled Flight* (Polity, 2023); translated by Stephen Muecke.

[8] *Face à Gaïa* (La Découverte, 2015). Published in English as *Facing Gaia* (Polity, 2017); translated by Catherine Porter.

[9] See *Facing Gaia* and *After Lockdown*.

is the sense in which 'we have never been modern', as Bruno proclaimed in his book of the same name.[10]

The living manufacture their own conditions of existence

But one discovery, possibly 'as important as that of Galileo in his time',[11] he said, was made by the British physiologist, chemist and engineer James Lovelock (1919–2022), author of *Gaia, a New Look at Life on Earth*:[12] living beings make their own conditions of existence. The atmosphere is not given, homeostatic, but produced by all the living beings that populate the Earth, as affirmed in her turn by the microbiologist Lynn Margulis (1938–2011).

And so, we live on this varnish, this fine skin a few kilometres thick that covers the terrestrial globe and that certain scientists, like geochemist Jérôme Gaillardet, professor at the Institut de physique du globe, Paris, call 'the critical zone'. An envelope on which we must now 'land', instead of living an uprooted existence, so as to maintain the conditions that make that envelope habitable, enabling life to continue. It's this envelope to which Bruno gives the name Gaia, taking up a scientific hypothesis but also a myth that comes down to us from Ancient Greece and that refers to 'the mother goddess', matrix of all the deities.

---

[10] *Nous n'avons jamais été modernes* (La Découverte, 1991). Published in English as *We Have Never Been Modern* (Harvard University Press, 1993); translated by Catherine Porter.
[11] See *Facing Gaia*.
[12] Oxford University Press, 1979.

For we have also changed cosmologies. The way we represent the world and the beings that surround us is no longer the same. In bringing planet Earth closer to the other celestial bodies, the Galilean revolution allowed us to go 'from a closed world to the infinite universe', as the philosopher of the sciences Alexandre Koyré (1892–1964) said.[13] Galileo looked up to the sky, Lovelock looked down to the ground. 'To complete the picture, we had to supplement Galileo's Earth that moves with Lovelock's Earth that is moved,' as Bruno sums it up.

This is why his philosophy allows us to think about the ecological crisis anew. But also to act so as to 'land on this new Earth'. How? Through self-description, which consists for each and every one of us as citizens in 'describing not where you live, but who you live off',[14] and in mapping the territory you depend on. His model? The lists of grievances of the French Revolution which provided the Third Estate with an opportunity precisely to depict their territory and allowed them to catalogue the inequalities they suffered. Because 'a people who know how to describe themselves are capable of reorienting themselves politically'.

His method? The inquiry, whose power he never ceased asserting and proving.[15] A pragmatist as a person and an empiricist as a philosopher, he teamed up with the consortium 'Où atterrir?' after the 'Gilets jaunes' crisis, and led a series of self-description workshops in France in La Châtre (Indre), Saint-Junien

---

[13] Alexandre Koyré, *From the Closed World to the Infinite Universe* (Johns Hopkins University Press, 1968).
[14] See *After Lockdown*.
[15] *Puissances de l'enquête* (Les Liens qui libèrent, 2022).

(Haute-Vienne), Ris-Orangis (Essonne), and Sevran (Seine-Saint-Denis). 'Who do you depend on to exist?' proved to be the central question that needs to be asked to 'go from inarticulate complaint to the grievance', the query needed so as to form new alliances.

This art of questioning was condensed into a 'questionnaire' in the form of an aid to the self-description experiment and launched during the first lockdown. It had a resounding effect, opening as it does with a question that got a lot of confined people thinking: 'What are some of the suspended activities that you would like to see *not* coming back?'[16]

A kind of collective thinking

'Où atterrir? (Where do we land?) is a fundamental research device just like others this collective thinker has never ceased putting in place, such as two recent exhibitions he curated. One of these, 'Critical Zones', was put together at the ZKM in Karlsruhe in 2020 with the collaboration of Austrian artist Peter Weibel; the other, 'Toi et moi, on ne vit pas sur la même planète' ('We don't live on the same planet, you and I), was mounted at the Centre Pompidou Metz, with Martin Guinard and Eva Lin.

Composed of installations and performances intended not to illustrate an idea or to stage a philosophy but to produce a 'thought experiment', these two shows hooked other disciplines up to artistic practices in an association that promoted reflection on the new cosmol-

---

[16] Cf. Bruno Latour, 'What protective measures can you think of so we don't go back to the pre-crisis production model?', translated by Stephen Muecke, AOC (29 March 2020).

ogy. 'I don't know how to solve certain questions I put to myself,' Bruno liked to say, 'so I appeal to experts who know more about it than I do, as well as to artists whose sensibility is very different, and the friction allows us to produce thought.'

It must be said that Bruno thinks in groups and reflects in teams, with the aid of collectives and collective experiments. Such as at Sciences Po, within several programmes he founded when he was the school's scientific director (2007–12), including: Medialab, an interdisciplinary laboratory created in 2009 which conducts research on the relations between the digital and societies and is currently directed by sociologist Dominique Cardon; SPEAP, a school of political arts launched in 2010, now headed by historian of the sciences and playwright Frédérique Aït-Touati, who staged an impressive performance-reading of Bruno's *Moving Earths* (2019).

Bruno also initiated an innovative masters course at Sciences Po, the Mapping Controversies project (or FORCCAST),[17] designed to analyse the sciences and technologies, and first run by sociologist Nicolas Benvegnu. This aims to explore and visualize the complexity of public debates which mash together issues that are every bit as social as spatial, every bit as geographic as scientific, as in the case of the controversy over invasive plant species, which he recently seized on.

He also launched Terra Forma, piloted notably by Alexandra Arènes and Axelle Grégoire, two young architects who link the issue of the landscape to territorial policy. Not to mention, of course, the 'Où atterrir?'

---

[17] An acronym for FORmation par la Cartographie des Controverses à l'Analyse des Sciences et des Techniques.

consortium, referred to above, in which Bruno worked, in particular, with the architect Soheil Hajmirbaba and composer Jean-Pierre Seyvos.

Work also went on at home *en famille*, with Chantal Latour, his wife, a musician, coordinator, mediator and artistic collaborator at S-composition, specializing in shared creative ateliers, and Chloé Latour, his daughter, a lawyer and theatre director who, along with Frédérique Aït-Touati, staged Bruno's play *Gaïa Global Circus* (2013). 'Not a firm, but a farm, with father, mother, and daughter,' he used to joke, while his son Robinson, for his part, has been pursuing his career as a scriptwriter.

Society doesn't exist

Watching Bruno co-animate these closely related groups and help map their attachments during sessions punctuated by moments of theatre and song was a gripping experience. For, despite his aura and his flashes of brilliance, the philosopher was never overbearing, but empathetic, attentive, totally immersed in these inquiries into our conditions of existence, these journeys of shared experiences.

If the collectives were so important to him, that was due to his conception of sociology, which he saw not as a science of the social, but as one of associations.[18] 'A society doesn't hold together on account of some superstructure, the collective holds together through

---

[18] *Changer de société, refaire de la sociologie* (La Découverte, 2006). Published in English as *Reassembling the Social: An Introduction to Actor-Network-Theory* (Oxford University Press, 2005).

collectors,' asserted the man behind actor-network theory,[19] which, within the historiography of the social sciences, was closer to a sociology of description (close to Gabriel Tarde) than to a sociology of explanation (derived from Émile Durkheim).

In one of his last classes at the Collège de France, Michel Foucault argued that we had to 'defend society'. Bruno explains that society doesn't exist, that it's not something given, and that we need 'to see the social as the new association between surprising beings that come along and shatter the comfortable certainty of belonging to a common world'. This is because the social is constantly changing, so other terrains and other methods of inquiry are called for. Hence the centrality of his *Enquête sur les modes d'existence*,[20] in which he demonstrates that there are several 'regimes of truth'.

Bruno didn't come to ecology via a practice as a naturalist or because of a strong penchant for wide open spaces and the wilderness, even if his Burgundian origins undoubtedly made him sensitive to the notions of *terroir* and territory. He came to it via the sociology of the sciences. In San Diego, at the Salk Institute, he had the luck to be there when endorphin was discovered by the team led by professor of endocrinology Roger Guillemin, who was awarded the Nobel Prize for Medicine in 1977.

The main thing Bruno observes is 'how an artificial place can establish accepted facts'. A long way from classical epistemology, he understands that science is a practice that doesn't set nature against culture or

---

[19] See *Reassembling the Social*.
[20] Published by La Découverte in 2012. Translated in English as *An Inquiry into Modes of Existence: An Anthropology of the Moderns* (Harvard University Press, 2013); translated by Catherine Porter.

certainty against opinion. Science is made of controversies; it is socially constructed.[21]

This heterodox ethnology of the sciences earned him the accusation of 'relativism', assuming he denied the existence of a scientific truth, whereas his sociology is 'relationist': it makes the connections between theoretical, empirical, social, and technical elements that allow us to attain a specific form of truth.

'An overdose of reductionism'

Bruno's method is the same for the law or religion. He is interested in regimes of veridiction: 'What does it mean to speak juridically?' 'What does it mean to speak religiously?' A way of homing in on circumstantial truths that's tightly linked to his philosophy thesis, defended in 1975 and entitled 'Exegesis and Ontology'. For Bruno philosophizes point by point, without skipping the mediating stages.

His encounter with philosophy, in his final year, converted him: 'I knew immediately that I'd be a philosopher,' he said. 'Because, paradoxically, the other branches of knowledge seemed to me to be more uncertain.' His reading of Nietzsche led him to smash idols, as you like to do at eighteen years of age, but especially to construct 'a merciless critique of the notion of a fundament'.

The critique constructed by Charles Péguy, both a Catholic and a socialist, stayed with him always, from

---

[21] *La vie de laboratoire. La Production des faits scientifiques*, with Steve Woolgar. (La Découverte, 1988). Originally published in English as *Laboratory Life: The Social Construction of Scientific Facts* (SAGE Publications, 1979); later editions dropped the word 'social'.

his early years as a militant in the Jeunesse étudiante chrétienne, or Young Christian Students, which he joined in the 1960s, right up to his very last essays devoted to political ecology:

> What once made him [Péguy] a reactionary, his writing about the Incarnation, his thinking about native soil and attachment, allows him to shed light on the situation we find ourselves in now, we who no longer know what space to inhabit. They talk about all these young people who're mobilizing out of fear of the ecological catastrophe. Well, Péguy had understood this: the modern world deprives us of our capacity to engender, and that loss is a tragedy.

And it's important to remember, along with the members of the *Laudata si'* chair of the Collège des Bernadins in Paris, that 'Pope Francis's prophetic appeal', launched in the encyclical of 2015, the year when *Face à Gaïa* appeared, was, for Bruno, 'a divine surprise'. In actual fact, as theologian Frédéric Louzeau, historian Grégory Quenet, and theologian Olric de Gélis explain,

> Bruno Latour immediately spotted the two major innovations of *Laudata si'*: the link between the Earth's devastation and social injustice, recognition of the power to suffer and to act of the Earth itself. He also registered that those two innovations were associated with the word 'clamour', which, in Latin as in French, has a legal origin: the Earth and the poor are lodging a complaint!

As a young teacher in Burgundy, Bruno had a revelation. A sort of epiphany. In 1972, on the road that links Dijon to Gray (Haute-Saône), he felt 'forced to stop' and pulled over on the verge, 'brought to my senses after an overdose of reductionism'. In effect, every one of us seeks to reduce the world that surrounds us to a principle, an idea, an opinion: 'A Christian,' he writes in *Irréductions,*

> loves a God who is capable of reducing the world to himself because he created it. . . . An astronomer looks for the origin of the universe by deducing its evolution from the Big Bang. A mathematician seeks axioms that imply all the others as corollaries and consequences. A philosopher hopes to find the radical foundation which makes all the rest epiphenomenal. . . . An intellectual strives to make the 'simple' practices and opinions of the vulgar explicit and conscious.[22]

Well, he realized on that day with its stark blue winter sky, 'Nothing can be reduced to anything else, nothing can be deduced from anything else, everything may be allied to everything else.' Such was his 'exorcism'. An 'exorcism', he wrote, that 'defeated demons one by one. It was a wintry sky, and very blue. I no longer needed to prop it up with a cosmology. . . . [F]or the first time in my life I saw things unreduced and set free.'[23] Such was the cosmology that oriented his whole philosophy. For if he was a sociologist by profession, he remained a philosopher till the end.

[22] Published by Métailié in 1984. Published in English in the second half of *The Pasteurization of France* (Harvard University, 1992), p. 162; translated by Alan Sheridan and John Law.
[23] See *The Pasteurization of France*, p. 163.

Introduction

Observing science

In this series of interviews Bruno did for Arté (the Franco-German cultural TV channel created in 1992),[24] he came out with this phrase, almost on a sob: 'Philosophy is so beautiful!' Why is this discipline, one capable of creating concepts, as Gilles Deleuze used to say, so beautiful, so powerful, and so intoxicating? 'I don't know how to answer that question,' Bruno said, 'except by crying. Philosophy – philosophers know this – is this totally amazing form that's interested in the totality, but that never attains it because the aim is not to attain it, but to love it.'[25] It's not saying much to say he loved that totality and sought to embrace it.

To begin with, in Côte d'Ivoire, where, having passed his *agrégation* (teacher's exam), he trained in anthropology. In Abidjan, more precisely, while he was doing his national service and had to teach Descartes's philosophy in a technical high school. An initial battleground where – already as a 'postcolonial' intellectual – he refused to pit a rational West against an Africa mired in irrationality. The experience allowed him to forge a 'symmetrical anthropology' that allowed him to study western societies the way ethnologues do African societies. This method eventually led him to observe a laboratory in California, and not just any old laboratory but the one run by a Nobel Prize winner. A decisive experience in understanding 'science in the making'.

---

[24] The text that follows this introduction is based on these interviews, which were conducted by Nicolas Truong in the autumn of 2021.
[25] See pp. 98–9 below.

Introduction

For Bruno Latour is a field-based intellectual. Even of history, since he had a passion for Pasteur and the history of the sciences.[26] He also had a passion for the history of technologies, which led him, in 1982, to join the Ecole des mines, where he remained for twenty-five years, notably at the Centre de sociologie et d'innovation, directed by Michel Caillon, who is behind actor-network theory.

This 'collective ferment' led to strikingly original research work, as attested by *Aramis ou l'amour des techniques*,[27] without question one of his favourite books, named after an automated metro line that nearly got built in the south of Paris. A book of 'scientifiction', a sociological inquiry doubled with 'the love story of a machine'.

In prefacing the book, Bruno sums up not only what it says, but also a research programme, a sociological method, a philosophical ambition and an ethical concern:

> I have sought to offer humanists a detailed analysis of a technology sufficiently magnificent and spiritual to convince them that the machines by which they are surrounded are cultural objects worthy of their attention and respect. ... I have sought to show technicians that they cannot even conceive of a technological object without taking into account the mass of human beings with all their passions and politics. ... Finally, I have sought to show researchers

---

[26] *Pasteur: guerre et paix des microbes* (Métailié, 1984); *Pasteur, une science, un style, un siècle* (Perrin, 1994). Both in *The Pasteurization of France*, cited above.

[27] Published by La Découverte in 1992. Published in English as *Aramis, or The Love of Technology* (Harvard University Press, 1996); translated by Catherine Porter.

in the social sciences that sociology is not the science of human beings alone – that it can welcome crowds of non-humans with open arms, just as it welcomed the working masses in the nineteenth century. Our collective is woven together out of speaking subjects, perhaps, but subjects to which poor objects, our inferior brothers, are attached at all points. By opening up to include objects, the social bond would become less mysterious.[28]

A 'new class struggle'

That makes it easier to understand why, in 1994, Bruno outlined a 'parliament of things' designed to 'bring into politics subjects rejected today on the part of science' and for a dialogue to be set up between representatives of humans and those of their 'non-human associates'. An indefatigable inventor of concepts, and an unmatchable initiator of percepts, Bruno made himself more political as the ecological emergency intensified.

'Ecology is the new class struggle,' he let fly in *Le Monde*,[29] on the publication of his book with Danish sociologist Nikolaj Schultz, *Mémo sur la nouvelle classe écologique*.[30] For conflicts are no longer exclusively social, but geosocial, they argue, before calling for a 'new ecological class' to proudly take up the torch borne by the socialists of last century.

Have his ideas triumphed? They've spread throughout the world, from the Belgian philosopher Vinciane

---

[28] *Aramis*, p. viii.
[29] 6 January 2022.
[30] Published by La Découverte in 2022. Published in English as *On the Emergence of an Ecological Class: A Memo* (Polity, 2022); translated by Julie Rose.

Despret to the American Anna Tsing, from the writer Richard Powers to the philosopher Donna Haraway, via the Indian essayist Amitav Ghosh. His books, the bulk of them published in Paris by La Découverte thanks to his collaboration with Philippe Pignarre, are translated into over twenty languages.

In France, his audience is vast. And the intellectuals he has taught, assisted, supported, are now read and commented on – people such as Frédérique Aït-Touati, political philosopher Pierre Charbonnier, feminist philosopher Emilie Hache, lawyer Sarah Vanuxem, theorist of metamorphoses Emanuele Coccia, philosopher of living beings and animal researcher Baptiste Morizot, art historian Estelle Zhong Mengual, philosopher and artist Matthieu Duperrex, anthropologist of animism Nastassja Martin, psychologist and photographer Émile Hermant, as well as anthropologist of the sciences and of health Charlotte Brives. Not to mention the poets and writers, such as Olivier Cadiot or Camille de Toledo, who has summed up the special quality of Bruno's mode of existence: 'the joy of thinking at the heart of the drama, the strength to yield neither to anguish nor to catastrophe'.[31] It's a constellation so ramified it's impossible to name them all.

A number of Bruno's students at Sciences Po copiloted the Citizens' Convention for the Climate, others work in local councils that have pivoted to ecology. With the anthropologist Philippe Descola, professor emeritus at the Collège de France, he brought about the ecopoliti-

---

[31] 'Ce que Bruno Latour nous laisse, en plus de toutes ses oeuvres, c'est son précieux mode d'existence', *Le Monde*, 22 October 2022. Translated as 'What Bruno Latour leaves us, in addition to all his works, is his precious mode of existence', *West Observer*, 19 October 2022.

cal turn in contemporary French thought as the chief of a clan he gathered together in his apartment in the rue Danton, Paris, where researchers and activists, writers and artists crossed paths. A bit like in the 18th-century salons where the philosophy of the Enlightenment broke out, you felt like you were meeting the new Diderots and d'Alemberts.

Bruno's 'diplomatic philosophy', notes Descola, especially since he branched out into the theme of the new climate regime and the issue of ecology, 'has become the thinking of the present moment', the thing that has made us 'become aware . . . that modernity set itself up in a cloud, way above ground, by claiming to separate humans from non-humans, nature from society'.[32]

'One day, perhaps, the age will be Deleuzian,' said Foucault in 1970, so impressed was he by the author of *Différence et répétition*.[33] Philosopher Patrice Maniglier today reckons that ours will be 'Latourian'. Or rather that 'it's not we that have become Latourians; it's our era'.[34] It would be contrary to the intuition of his youth to reduce Bruno Latour to a turn of phrase.

Particularly as, in recent times, he used to take his elegant, tall, and lanky figure for strolls around a world in flames, like some monsieur Hulot able to poetically inhabit the Age of the Anthropocene, and persuaded,

[32] Philippe Descola, 'Ta pensée audacieuse est devenue la pensée du temps présent', *Le Monde* (3 November 2022).

[33] Published by Presses Universitaires de France in 1968. Published in English as *Difference and Repetition* (Columbia University Press, 1994); translated by Paul Patton.

[34] Patrice Maniglier, 'Tout ce que vous avez voulu savoir sur Bruno Latour sans jamais oser le demander au SARS-CoV-2 – un moment latourien', *AOC* (21 April 2021).

like William James, that 'the Universe is a pluriverse'. Bruno knew the new situation better than anybody: 'My father, my grandfather could take their retirement, grow old quietly, die in peace: the summers of their childhood and those of their grandchildren could look alike,' he wrote.[35] 'Of course, the climate was fluctuating, but it didn't accompany the ageing of a generation the way it accompanies mine, that of the baby boomers. I can't take my retirement, grow old and die leaving my grandchildren a month of Augusts that can be detached from the story of my generation.'

It's because of this that at the end of these interviews, in the manner of a coda, Bruno addresses a letter to his grandson, to the generation that will turn 40 in 2060. Not by way of a conclusion, for, as Flaubert used to say, 'stupidity lies in wanting to draw conclusions', but as an opening, a salute to the future, an invitation to project ourselves, in spite of everything, into the future. The philosopher offers us an extraordinary tool kit here, one designed not only to fuel our reflection, but also to help us imagine new modes of living and acting. An invitation 'to become earthbound' by showing an empathy with the Earth that he called 'geopathy'. Bruno, then, has touched down. But he lives on, just like his oeuvre, irreducible.

[35] 'Un bel et épouvantable été', Le Monde (3 September 2016).

Changing worlds

Nicolas Truong: Bruno Latour, thank you for welcoming us into your home, in Paris, into this apartment where you live and where you've been working for many a long year. Why have you agreed to this series of interviews?

Bruno Latour: To start with, because I'm getting on a bit, and that's the moment when you look back at what you've done. After that, because, to all appearances, I've taken an interest in very diverse subjects such as the sciences, the law, fiction, and have done so using slightly bizarre methods. It's hard to follow: in bookshops, they never really know where to put my books. They put the one about Paris in the tourism section, another one will be in the philosophy of the sciences, a third in law . . . You're giving me the opportunity to explain my general argument, so that people can then throw themselves into those books without getting the feeling I'm spreading myself too thin. I'm happy about that because I haven't spread myself much at all. I've followed a line from beginning to end, and now it's time to be able to clarify that.

NT: Sociologist and anthropologist of the sciences and technologies, but above all every inch the philosopher, you're known to the general public notably through two of your books devoted to ecology. Delivered in the form of questions in the original French *Où atterrir?* in 2017[1] and *Où suis-je?* in 2021,[2] both present the idea that, in your view, we've changed worlds, that we no longer inhabit the same Earth. What is this change, and why don't we inhabit the same Earth any more?

BL: The problem is to do with dramatizing a situation. The political and ecological situation we're in is extraordinarily tough on everyone. We're plainly affected by all these transformations they tell us about every day in the papers: the issue of the climate, of these international gatherings to try to control biodiversity, and even the question of what progress and wealth are. We realize these issues are associated with the world we were in until recently: a world organized around the principle that things have no power to act. Galileo is a completely typical example of that world: taking an inclined plane and calculating the fall of billiard balls and that magnificent invention of the law of falling bodies, gravity. A billiard ball has no identity whatsoever, no power to act – what's known in English as agency. The billiard ball obeys laws, which are calculable and which Science, with a capital S, discovers.

---

[1] *Down to Earth* (2018).
[2] *After Lockdown: A Metamorphosis* (2021).

Changing worlds

We were accustomed to thinking that the world was made like this of things and beings that don't have the same agency. The great British philosopher [Alfred North] Whitehead called this the 'bifurcation of nature'. That's the idea that, dating from a certain era, round about the 17th century, the world was structured by a break between, on the one hand, the things that are true, known by the sciences but inaccessible outside the sciences, and, on the other, living things, people's subjectivity, the way they imagine this world, as well as their impressions of seeing perfectly magnificent things. All that we feel, we humans and living beings, is subjectively interesting, but it isn't what the world is made of. The world of bifurcation – that was the great definition of the previous world, which to simplify I call the modern world, and whose anthropology has always interested me.

But even if it seems strange to say that about the sciences, what we're dealing with is a problem of metaphysics. The metaphysical basis of the world we're in, in which we find ourselves, is a world of living things, made of life. In my opinion, it's this world – which certainly looks like it's made of life, and which we're discovering more and more with the earth sciences and analysis of living things and biodiversity – that the current situation makes blindingly obvious, with Covid and climate change. The world we need to land on, somehow, the world which we find ourselves situated in, is a world of viruses. Both on a small scale, of a virus that attacks humans, and on a large one, because the atmosphere we're comfortable in and the oxygen that allows us to breathe are also of viral and bacterial origin. Their mutations inevitably change the composition, the consistency, of the world we're in. Viruses and bacteria: these are the big operators that have transformed the Earth and made its history, the history that constructs the envelope of habitability we're situated inside. We don't even know, anyway, if viruses are alive. There's a whole series of enigmas about how they evolve: we don't know if they're foreign to us, if they're enemies or friends. But luckily we're covered in viruses and bacteria! If we weren't, we wouldn't be able to live.

If people are disoriented by the ecological issue and can't quite react rapidly to a situation everyone knows is catastrophic, this is largely due to the fact that they continue to be in the world of before, a world of objects that have no agency and that are controllable through calculation, a world of adaptable sciences, a world of the wealth and comfort provided by the system of production. But that's not the world we're in any more now, and it's in this sense that we've changed worlds. We're emerging from a world made of objects, things known by the sciences, where ideas of our own are subjective ideas about them. And then there's the other world we're entering, as living beings surrounded by other living beings, who do a heap of bizarre things and who react very rapidly to our actions. So I dramatize: 'We're no longer in the situation we were in before.' But it's my job to dramatize, to name things. There's a real difference to take note of. In the first case, there are no worries. We're in a world of relatively simple objects. They're going to obey our laws. In the other, we ask ourselves, on the contrary: 'What's this virus doing? How's it going to move around, to evolve?'

Changing worlds

NT: You often say that this shift in worlds that we're living through today is a revolution comparable to the Galilean revolution. Have we moved on in relation to what we imagined of the great cosmology of the Moderns?

BL: Yes, if we see cosmology, the way anthropologists would, as a distribution of powers to act, as a definition of the gods, a definition of who has agency and who doesn't. The Moderns, too, had a cosmology, which enabled their total, global expansion. To simplify, it's a very particular cosmology based on division, on distinction between a 'world of objects', to put it the way Philippe Descola does, and a subject who is in a way distant. When we take the climate and viruses into account, it's all over: no one can say now that there are subjects at a distance from the world they find themselves in. Through a surprising feedback loop, the action of humans at a certain place creates, for themselves and for humans in other places, living conditions that are uninhabitable. The cosmology in which subjective humans, subjects, could place themselves in a world that was remote, as was the case with Kant – that's a version typical of the Moderns but it's just not possible.

What does this mean? That the problem now is the problem of the subject. That's what interests me philosophically. What is a subject? What is the human subject of ecology? It's not the same subject as before. It doesn't have the possibility of doing the same things. It doesn't have access to the same confidence in objects. It's captured by a whole heap of forces that manipulate it from all sides. Stunningly, this is borne out at the minuscule level of the virus and of the medical issue, every bit as much as at the global level of the conditions of existence we find ourselves in, since the atmospheric conditions, the conditions of food and temperature, are themselves the unintentional product of these living things. I insist once more on this because it's the great novelty of the Earth system sciences. This is where we can talk about a second scientific revolution.

People talk today about fungi, lichens, microbiota ... Everyone's interested in living things. Even if it's sometimes a bit over the top, that remains a very significant symptom. We're starting to say to ourselves that in the end we're no longer in a world of objects we're distant from, but in amongst beings that overlap with us. This is true as far as viruses are concerned, but it's also very interesting to think about in relation to politics. It means our own existence intervenes and has an influence on all the others. In a world of objects that you could stack alongside each other, the possibilities for action seem infinite. And we Moderns have done amazing things this way. But if you're surrounded by beings that are all composed and superimposed, without ever knowing exactly if they're friends or enemies, and with which we're going to have to come to some agreement, it's just not the same world – especially as they're providing the living conditions we find ourselves in ... Once again, we need to make the comparison, draw a parallel with what's happened since 1610, that Galileo moment that's so important to history, and right up to the 1940s. That's a long transformation of our affects, our hopes, of the period we were about to go back to, of what we can expect from moral questions, expect from human action, from subjectivity. It's reassuring that all that was invented, because if we were capable of doing that, of undergoing the enormous transformation that was the first scientific revolution and that of the modern world, then we can start again now. We got ourselves out of all that, so we can get ourselves out of things now too. But it means a colossal amount of work.

NT: You consider that 'deep down, people know perfectly well that they've switched worlds and that they now inhabit a different Earth'. And, to that end, you like to cite the historian Paul Veyne: 'The great upheavals are sometimes as simple as the movement a sleeper makes turning over in bed.'[3]

BL: Yes, that's a lovely phrase of Veyne's. When we draw up the list of all the issues we're going to have to solve if we're going to get used to a world that's ecologized, not modernized, it's dizzying: it means so many transformations. Not just transformations of the energy system or the supply system, but also a transformation of moral questions, questions to do with defining topics, with property law . . . It's pretty overwhelming. Such a shift seems impossible. A lot of people think we can't do anything; there are sceptics, whether they're paid by the lobby groups or not . . . Nevertheless, the new spirit of the times is to feel we've changed worlds.

[3] See Latour and Schultz, *On the Emergence of an Ecological Class*, p. 84.

The end of modernity

NT: Why have we never been modern and what are Moderns, for you?

BL: When people say 'modern', there's usually this injunction implied: 'Modernize yourselves.' People want to systematically modernize the university, modernize the state, modernize agriculture . . . It's helpful to grasp that this watchword organizes the direction of history, through the fact of saying: we're advancing, the modernization front is inevitable, and it moves forward in this way. Behind us, all is archaism. And that, too, is inevitable: as soon as someone says to you: 'Modernize yourselves', you're immediately thrown into a panic situation: 'If I miss the train of modernization, I'll be . . .'

NT: Left behind.

BL: Eliminated. 'And if I remain on my guard, I become a reactionary, I become anti-modern.' You're then accused of archaism, accused of slowing down the path of progress and holding on to old values. But what does it mean, putting things that way? What are people hoping to gain by saying: 'Modernize yourselves'? Those are questions that were also posed by Covid. While it was claimed a great economic movement was going to go on growing, everything suddenly stopped. Everyone, each one at home, realized that in just a few weeks that enormous machine of development and progress could be paused, and people started to wonder finally: 'What are we looking for? What do we want?'

I'm not at all anti-modern, because saying, 'As for me, *I'm* resisting, *I'm* deliberately archaic, reactionary,' would be a way of accepting the modernization front. What we're dealing with here is most definitely an injunction: a term that defines a movement of history, only that history is not the one we're actually in. I see my contribution as studying and seeing the modern no longer as a catchword, but as an object of research – and turning the old injunction into a conundrum.

'Modern' was the slogan and rallying cry for organizing the modernization front, which is nearing its end since we're realizing just now that it's a front of destruction. A lot of people today agree to consider that we're not going to go as far as modernizing the planet. If we modernize it, it disappears. It becomes uninhabitable and unliveable for us human beings. These days, you can be believed when you say what I was saying thirty years ago: we've finished off modernity. It's a parenthesis, a moment in history that's reached its use-by date. I like to say that we need 'to accept being like Orsay'[1] when Beaubourg[2] was set

---

[1] The Musée d'Orsay.
[2] The Centre Pompidou.

up. It's a very interesting thing, a museum of modernity! But only provided we stop always wanting to go on being modern, and create the museum required by the now passed moment of modernity.

What's been the good of the 20th century? I'm still setting myself that problem. I've chalked up fifty years of studies, and as I've gone along I've become aware that there is no subject that's clarified by the fact of stating what is modern and what isn't. There isn't a single subject, especially in the history of the sciences. People try to define the Moderns as those who believe in the bifurcation between subjectivity and objectivity, those who finally understood the difference between opinion, culture, on the one hand, and nature, on the other. But if you try to apply this separation, you only have to study the history of technologies or the sciences to notice they've done exactly the opposite. The Moderns are the people who mashed up, in the most extreme – sometimes also the most magnificent – way, politics, science, technology, the law, in their empire. That's a big surprise: they never stop doing the opposite of what they claim. This sort of thing just isn't said any more, but I really like this expression you hear in Westerns: 'White man speaks with forked tongue.' It's true, it's a really beautiful expression. The Moderns are inauthentic. They speak with forked tongues, they always do the opposite of what they say. They're always out of true in relation to what they do, and in the 1920s, they really go at it hammer and tongs, they exaggerate in their exaggeration, in their inauthenticity.

In '89, as I was working on this issue, the [Berlin] Wall came down. That event entailed a kind of tremendous reaction of enthusiasm at the triumph of liberalism. So then for me there's something every bit as extraordinary as the event of the fall of the Wall: the complete incomprehension that that event was triggered by liberalism. That was the moment of maximum acceleration, maximum extractivism, and maximum denial. We'd been accelerating ever since the war, but at the fall of the Wall, we escaped into the acceleration of acceleration. I was very surprised, because if we do indeed see the Soviets collapse in '89, we also witness the beginning of all the big conferences in Tokyo, Rio, on ecology. It's shattering: from the point of view of the ecological issue, it was both the moment when we could have acted on it, the ideal opportunity to address the real issue, the one that was to become what we call 'the new climate regime', and at the same time the moment of maximum denial of it. That's also the enigma of the history of the 20th century: it constantly denied the situation it found itself in.

NT: That modern moment is equally modern from an aesthetic point of view. Rimbaud says notably: 'We must be absolutely modern.' We've got ourselves out of that, but what world did we get ourselves into?

BL: The phrase 'modernize yourselves' had enormous power, but also hid its complexity, harshness, and cruelty as a slogan. Since the '50s, 'modernize yourselves' in reality means: 'abandon your past and separate yourself from the Earth', if we're to simplify the process. We 'take off'! I recall that in the '50s, everyone was supposed to 'take off'. The so-called developing countries 'took off'. It was the whole idea of taking off. That mantra remains very important because we don't have any alternative. So, to answer your question, that's what we've got to work on: what's the alternative to modernity? Take wealth, freedom, emancipation; without modernity, what do they look like? The alternative is what I call 'ecologizing'. No one has an exact idea of what that means, precisely because it's an enormous shift in the definition of time, of its passing, of the separation between past and future. The separation between past and future can't be made clear-cut by saying that what's on the wrong side of the modernization front is finished, and what's on the other side is unified and steaming ahead. Modernizing or ecologizing are probably totally opposed ... But ecologizing implies something of the order of composing.

Composing, in the proper sense of the term, completely freely, with formulae that belong to the past, the future, and the present. We need to free ourselves from the enormous pressure of modernization, which completely blinds us when it comes to making decisions and choices; we need to be able to choose, to distinguish good technology from bad technology, good law from bad law. Our capacities to choose – which is what I call composing – are different, profoundly different, from what people meant by modernizing. They can't be rallied under one great slogan! It's not enough to hear ourselves say: 'Compose your life so it's in tune with the planet's habitability', in order to mobilize ourselves immediately in a certain order. Rather, we start by asking ourselves: 'So, what do I do? Permaculture on the one hand ... And I'd still like to ditch CO_2 ... But how do I go about it?' That's the way we get back into this world, this world we live in, made up of infinite controversies about how we can change our ways of living. But that's healthy! Because what's so terrible in the expression 'modernizing' is that it blinds us. It completely prevents you from asking yourself questions about what you're going to leave behind.

I'll take one example, which may be minuscule but is very exciting and which interested my students a lot: hedges. People either love them or hate them. There are modern hedges, which have generally been eradicated, there are postmodern hedges, and lastly there are hedges that are composed, mixed. I'm not talking about the return of the hedge and of traditional small-scale farming, which made the peasants every bit as miserable and required enormous labour from them. I'm talking about a composite hedge. Today, lots of people are working on hedges: biologists, naturalists, new peasants who once again call themselves 'peasants' because they're not farmers any more.

That's what 'composing' is, and it goes for all topics.

The alternative message of composition means diving headlong into controversies; abandoning the separation between what's progress and what's archaic; getting interested obviously in the fundamental question of habitability; and getting liveability standards to take precedence over questions of production. That takes work! We've never been modern, but we've got away from the idea that we were. The construction site remains completely open.

NT: It's a world, a composite construction site, based on composition, recomposition.

BL: Composing is a really beautiful term because it's also musical. It's about arrangements, negotiations, *modus vivendi*. We can see why we also need to abandon the idea that politics is going to be modern. Modern politics is the brand that says where we have to go and how the order has to be given; but we need a modest politics for these composite arrangements. We also need a modest science, because science is going to be groping its way through heaps of controversies if it's going to succeed in saying what has to be done. And we need a modest practical technology, capable of telling itself: 'I invent a technique, so there are unexpected consequences, so there's a controversy, so it's local, and so we're going to have to argue.' A whole society has to acquire a critical faculty which it's been deprived of by the idea of modernity. By being modest in all these different modes, society has to finally see that we're going to need to create an 'ecological' civilization based on a simple composition. And that's what's exciting: we've never been modern, but the fact of believing we are continues to have effects that are extraordinarily powerful.

Gaia puts us on notice

NT: We're literally living in orbit, you say, and today we need to land. Landing means living in what scientists call the 'critical zone', living on Gaia, with Gaia. Gaia is both a concept developed by James Lovelock,[1] the British physiologist and engineer, and a myth that comes to us from Antiquity, from Greek mythology. Gaia is the mother goddess, the matrix of all the deities. While we know that the catastrophe is there, that the UN's scientists and experts tell us so in every new report, why do you need Gaia to get us out of the state of impotence we find ourselves in? What does recourse to that particular entity mean for describing what's happening to us and for mobilizing the citizens of this new ecological class you're pinning your hopes on?

BL: If I'd wanted to simplify things, I wouldn't have used Gaia. Gaia has really complicated my life. The

---

[1] James Lovelock was still alive when this interview took place in the autumn of 2021. He died on 26 July 2022.

idea Lovelock invented is of a simplicity as extreme as the discovery he made in the '60s that the atmosphere is not in thermodynamic balance. There's no reason for the atmosphere to be 30% oxygen, since oxygen reacts with everything; it ought to have disappeared a long time ago. Lovelock has recounted the celebrated episode in the course of which he compares our atmosphere with that of Mars and says: 'It's not worth the trouble of going to Mars, gentlemen biologists. You want to send my instruments there' – because he used to make instruments – 'but I know there is no life up there.' They continue to look for life on Mars, but there is no Gaia up there. There is no planet completely transformed by living things for billions of years. And if there ever had been at a given moment, we might perhaps find some cells somewhere, but that moment has passed.

There is no Gaia in the sense of an envelope, or in the sense of this physico-chemical transformation of the Earth's conditions, which weren't initially all that favourable, into favourable conditions. That particular transformation is due to the fact that living beings aren't just organisms in an environment, but have the particularity of transforming the environment to their benefit. That's not out of generosity or friendliness, but simply out of interconnection. This is what's so very important: the interconnection of living beings among themselves. A living being has a metabolism. It absorbs heaps of weird things and the weird things it spits out again are used by others as opportunities. It takes four billion years, but it's this recycling that ends up creating conditions we can take advantage of. This is where the fundamental question of the new cosmology intervenes, the question of the habitability of the planet. The question of how it was made habitable, how it's been kept habitable, and how we fight those who are making it uninhabitable. And Gaia is a beautiful name! It's important that it's a myth, and that it's a scientific, mythological, and political concept all at the same time. It's precisely because the term is beyond hybrid that it's also clearly the name for a change in cosmology. Gaia is a magnificent term. But a lot of people call their dogs Gaia, which is annoying!

NT: Their children too!

BL: Or their children, but that's not quite as bad. Gaia really is a brilliant idea. Lovelock has often told this story: he finds himself in a village pub, having a beer with his friend William Golding, author of *Lord of the Flies*, and he explains his extraordinary idea of the self-regulation of the planet. Golding tells him it's a fantastic idea, one that deserves to be given a striking name. He suggests Gaia. Lovelock doesn't really understand what's being said to him because he's not schooled in the humanities – he's illiterate in Latin and Greek – but he adopts the term in the end.

That's a truly major historical event, absolutely fascinating. A Nobel Prize winner in Literature, who's a physicist himself, what's more, suggests a decisive term to Lovelock, physiologist and chemist. How do you expect a philosopher like me to overlook an episode like that?! It's an extraordinary conjunction, a conjunction that's about to expand further thanks to the fact that Lovelock would become very close friends with Lyn Margulis, who actually worked on viruses and bacteria and on the long-term history of the Earth. Margulis was particularly interested in bacteria, and Lovelock in the macro elements in the atmosphere. To simplify, he was a specialist in the very fine collecting of quantities of gas, and had also done work on the ozone layer. They meet up and in the early '70s they form this concept of Gaia together.

And then there's what Isabelle Stengers calls the intrusion of Gaia. She's less concerned with the question of understanding the science of Gaia, which interests me a lot, than with the total surprise of saying: 'We're in a different world.' The Gaia of Isabelle Stengers is a character who impacts policy.

We're inside Gaia. The question of its conditions of habitability has become essential. We're no longer in the old world where the most important question was using resources in order to grow. For that reason, we can't separate mythology, science, and politics. That's not what a cosmology is. A cosmology is the connection between these things. When an anthropologist studies the cosmology of the Baruya[2] or the Yanomami,[3] they don't separate what's political, the way the society's organized, and the question of whether there are gods. All of that is inevitably linked. And us? How could we claim to change cosmologies without giving a name to this new situation?

I declare that Gaia is the name of the new situation. Precisely because it's mythological, it's scientific, it's political. That's highly problematic; the term 'critical zone' which you used earlier is a calmer term. Critical zone is a term created by my friends. It's not a very

[2] A New Guinea tribe.
[3] A scattered Amazonian tribe.

widespread term, but in America and in France this notion is used to designate exactly the same thing: the fact that our experience is that of living beings surrounded by living beings, inside a world manufactured by living beings. That's minuscule compared to the notions people entertained in the previous period of what a planet is. The terrestrial globe includes a whole series of things we don't experience. Even if there are instruments for knowing what there is, we don't go to the centre of the Earth to find out how it works, because we're not 'in' the planet. We're on the varnish, the ultra-thin varnish of this Earth. That surface of a few kilometres – that's the critical zone.

NT: It's the space that encircles, that encompasses planet Earth. So how big is it?

BL: It's nothing much at all, but it's what's interesting. What we live off, what we have experience of, is both the only thing we've experienced, as living beings surrounded by other living beings, and at the same time nothing much. In the old world, we placed ourselves in planet Earth; we went to Mars, we wanted to go into space and we were fascinated by it. The old cosmology was that of the infinite universe, and we felt like we were faced with that infinity. Suddenly we find ourselves back inside a minuscule zone, which we share and which has been manufactured by living beings for four billion years. Our actions as industrialized humans inevitably take up enormous room, which was not what was anticipated because three centuries ago, and right up till the pre-war years, the trace humans left on planet Earth was negligible. Compared to the infinite universe we were in before, humans are practically nothing. The Earth system hadn't entered into our regime of action and so didn't come into politics, either. People were transforming the environment in the sense of the landscape, but not the Earth system and not our conditions of living in the universe. The difference is that in the critical zone living conditions have been profoundly altered. The term thus allows us to more easily grasp the fact that it's nothing more than this tiny space scientists study and which we live inside. In this particular world, humans count enormously. It's a lockdown. And that fact of suddenly finding ourselves locked down in a world that's nothing much from the point of view of the universe, but inside which the capacity of industrialized humans to alter the habitability is significant: that makes this question of habitability the fundamental concept.

Among the other major notions currently under discussion, there's the notion of the Anthropocene, which allows our friends who are working on it to count the influence of industralized humans on the rest of the planet. It's a lot of fun to compare the weight of humans as many scientists are now doing. They show, for instance, that bulldozers move more earth than so-called natural erosion, and that these humans who are nothing in terms of weight become substantial in terms of transforming power, to the point of being, as they say, a major 'geological force'. That's where the notion of the Anthropocene is right, and these problems of scale are what makes the question of politics so fundamental.

So then, why do we need Gaia? We need to turn to it because, after all, there are a certain number of complex things to take in. Industrialized humans count for a lot, but the critical zone is still nothing much at the same time. We need to understand that the environment is made by living beings and not, as we believed before, that living beings occupy an environment they adapt to. Life itself, from a physicist's point of view, is also nothing much at all in terms of energy. And yet it has transformed everything: minerals, mountains, the atmosphere. It has transformed the conditions of existence we find ourselves in. It's so strange: it's nothing much and yet there are such major consequences. That's why these concepts are complex. And then again, since nothing serious about the Earth sciences is actually taught, people wonder where they are. 'Where are we?', the question of the world we find ourselves in, becomes a fundamental question. There are so many things that have been transformed that we have to be able to name this. That's where I dramatize things, for philosophers who do their job have to give names to these things: where we are is inside Gaia.

Where do we land?

NT: Knowing how to describe yourself, and notably to answer the question: 'Who or what do I depend on to exist and subsist?', is in your view essential for us to be able to land. Becoming aware not only of the world we live in, but equally of the world we live off. How can this practice allow us to find some kind of orientation in politics today?

BK: The crucial political phenomenon of the previous age was, once again: how is it that an entire civilization, confronted by a threat they were perfectly aware of, did not react?

The problem is that ever since the '80s, we've been disoriented and we don't even know why we don't act. We could say it's because of the lobbyists, that too many things are against it, and that's also true. But the inaction is so massive we probably need to look for other reasons for it.

I propose we put the problem this way: 'How do you expect people to react rapidly to such a fundamental change in cosmology?' And the solution to this problem, as I've proposed it, is to go back to basics. What I call 'basics' means writing down on a bit of paper what the situation is that you find yourself in. That way we introduce the question of territory. It's a notion that might look simple or superficial, but there's a small variation: the territory isn't where you are in the sense of geographical coordinates, but what you depend on – because dependence has become the fundamental issue. The previous world was founded on the issue of emancipation. In this new world where you are right now, the fundamental problem is that you depend, and that what you depend on defines who you are. That's completely different from the previous version: we're feeling our way in a world we don't know.

If we want to give ourselves the means to get to know this new world, we have to acquire an apparatus to describe it. Not describe it objectively as if someone outside it told you that you were in another world, but describe it for yourself. It might seem strange, but I'm obsessed with description. Describing also means sitting down, parking yourself, having a seat. For any fundamental question of philosophy and ontology, I always look for a solution that we might call practical, empirical. The solution I've found for this is: 'List your dependencies. You are what you depend on.' Or rather: 'What you depend on will define a territory.' So, that's what I try to put in place.

Why is this interesting from a political point of view? Because for the moment, in the actual state of things, our political opinions are associated with the previous world. So we need to redescribe, and say: 'We're sorry, but your political opinions don't interest us.' That's a simple way of expressing the proposal I'm making.

NT: I've had an opportunity to follow a few of the workshops involving your consortium, Où atterrir? In these self-description workshops you conduct in Saint-Junien in the Haute-Vienne, in Ris-Orangis, and also in Sevran, you ask participants to designate the entity they depend on to exist and which now finds itself under threat. You also call that 'the stone in your shoe'.

BL: It's a weapon against the expression of opinions. When you ask people to talk politics, they always think they've got to rise to a very high level of generality. They get into a position, close to Rousseau's, which is to abandon your own point of view and take on that of the general will. Severing all your own ties so as to participate in the will of the people as a whole – that's the very definition of political expression according to Rousseau.

NT: 'Let us lay aside all the facts.'

BL: Let us lay aside the *cliques*, let us block all influence on the expression of opinions, in order finally to obtain the general will. That has never made any sense and it makes even less sense in the current situation. So we need to go right back to basics, to first base . . . The base of the base – that's our feet! And at our feet there are stones that are hurting us. John Dewey has a very nice expression: 'The man who wears the shoe knows best that it pinches and where it pinches.'[1] Talking about where our foot hurts allows us to avoid soaring off into generality too rapidly.

---

[1] John Dewey, *The Public and Its Problems: An Essay in Political Inquiry* (Gateway Books, 1946 [1927]), p. 207.

Where do we land?

I haven't lost my obsession with the notion of a collective. A 'collective' is something you have to 'collect'. If it's not collected properly, you won't be able to express anything. So it's not about replacing your own opinion with that of social networks or whatever's doing the rounds; that wouldn't allow people to work out where they are. In the workshops, we start again with what hurts rather than with general problems. For instance, one of our stockbreeder friends begins his description in the mode of the FNSEA,[2] to which he belongs, and in the mode of trade unionists who champion his own position by attacking the agricultural machine. This is where we need to intervene and say, 'No, that's not it. Make your list of all the beings you depend on.' Description doesn't happen all by itself: we need very intense mechanisms to put pressure on people to get it right.

By doing his description again, our friend realizes he depends on a lot of things that are under threat, particularly where he lives in the Limousin.[3] He depends on the CAP,[4] which is in the process of being rewritten somewhere in Brussels. He depends on suppliers and wonders whether he could perhaps do without what those suppliers sell him. But how? He starts rewriting on his own the list of all the things he depends on . . . We have to help him. And because he sees the way the others react, he manages to reconsider his situation: 'Actually, I can inhabit a different territory from the one I'm in,' a territory in the sense

---

[2] Fédération nationale des syndicats d'exploitants agricoles, or farmers' union.
[3] In southwest France.
[4] Common Agricultural Policy.

that I defined it a moment ago. At the end of a year, this stockbreeder is launched on something like a revolution, a metamorphosis; and even though he's still in the FNSEA, he has completely transformed his farm.

Why? Because description allows you to visualize situations that can thus be strung together. That's what interested me in this 'Où atterrir' business: it's a really tiny core sampling, a minuscule example, but it's on that pinhead that we do the fundamental research. I keep repeating myself, but it's important to say one more time that my model is that of the lists of grievances: the fact that the description of a situation of injustice, on a territory whose composition you spell out, reveals the possibility of making complaints to institutions, to the state – or to the King at the time – and to propose profound changes to its administration. If you don't know what the territory is you inhabit, the demands you might address to the administration probably won't make any kind of sense to it. But since we've changed territories, the administration now has to tell itself that the administrative system that we put in place to modernize France after the war is itself no longer fit for purpose.

There is no ecological government. We don't know what ecological model would bring about wealth, freedom, maintain emancipation, and yet be able to stick within the lockdown envelope – the envelope of habitability. No one has any real sense of it, no more in America than in Germany. And yet thousands of people are trying and feeling their way in this business. The idea I lay claim to, which 'Où atterrir?'

allowed me to validate in the minuscule core sample we took, is that we need to begin, each one of us for ourselves, by proceeding the way they did at the time of the Revolution. It's a lot harder today, though, because any description of the world we depend on is vastly more complexified by three centuries of economic history and particularly by globalization. It's stating the bleeding obvious, but when you're living in the Limousin, or in Brittany, or anywhere else, you depend on a world that's very removed from you. For instance, soya from Brazil is essential to Breton pigs. If I'm in Brittany, I can't ignore this world I depend on by saying that's a matter for Brazil while I deal with Bretons. If I accept that I have to try to understand, to reconcile the two, the political task is then completely different. The questions that emerge when you describe the things you depend on place an extraordinary constraint on the political question.

That's how what I call classes, not social classes in the traditional sense of the term but geo-social classes, appeared; when you allow, say, the question of Brazil to erupt inside Brittany. If we're starting to understand the issues of habitability in Brittany, we have to go through soya to Brazil. For people reduced to asking themselves: 'But what can *I* do down there?', there is undeniably something overwhelming. Those who do this exercise weren't necessarily any less overwhelmed, but physically they weren't the same, because the awareness made possible by the description process also re-creates capacities for action. That's what especially interested us in the 'Où atterrir?' experiment: the fact of being able to say to yourself that if I'm able to do things on my small scale, then I have the power to act after all, since the small scale is what the world is made of.

When you recommence the work of description, you get away from the thing that's the sin of, or at least spells disaster for, any political discussion: the idea that we have to systematically base ourselves on the next level, and move on to another regime of generality. Politics isn't about changing levels of generality, it's about following the network of our dependencies and our affiliations as far as it goes. We're not doing this exercise for therapeutic reasons, but it undeniably has the effect of giving people back, restoring, their political capacities. Obviously, it's at a pretty small level, but the big is made up entirely of the small. And what the magnificent example the Covid crisis showed us is that this pretty small, spluttering virus managed to take over the whole globe in just three weeks. That's a nice model of composing the big from the multiple connections of the small.

The new ecological class

NT: To combat the devastation of the planet, you say we need to foster the emergence of new geo-social classes that have interests in common. This ecological class, which you're counting on, would be proud of itself and capable of taking up the fight through alliances with individuals, groups, and entities that it would never have associated with in the past.

BL: Yes, that's an even more fictional and speculative proposal than the rest. I mean, does it exist, this ecological class? Once again, I'm doing my work as a philosopher, which is to anticipate, to name something we sense. At the point we're at now, we get the feeling that ecological questions have become the equivalent of the political questions of yore, meaning the ones it's legitimate and interesting to fight over. But our affiliations and associations aren't the same any more. That's what I mean by the advent of a new class. Not in the traditional, Marxist-inspired sense of social classes, but more in the sense meant by Norbert Elias, one of the great sociologists and historians of civilization: classes based on culture.

There will definitely come a time when the question of ecology will be central, and it's in that particular culture that the associations and divides between friends and enemies are going to define themselves. It remains complicated for the moment, because we don't really know. There are disputes over every topic, like the question of wind turbines. There's no ecological issue that isn't a contentious affair. So we need to form battlefronts – we definitely do meet up with the old definition of classes here. But this time round the battlefronts won't hold together just over the liberal and socialist questions of production and the distribution of the goods produced, to summarize quickly, but over questions of habitability. These are absolutely new and difficult political problems that we've never set ourselves before this. Not for a single second did our predecessors worry about asking themselves, as we have to do for every decision we make, if they should also worry about the temperature of the atmosphere. They would obviously have been interested in drought, in the disappearance of forests and in other things, but not in the atmosphere. That would never have been taken into consideration. Now, we have to get it into the detail of our decisions.

We need to bear in mind that what I call the geo-social classes are still forming. It's clear that the ecological issue is becoming the most crucial issue; but there are people who deny it, and also people who don't know how to assimilate it. It's also in these ways of relating to it that we can see we're currently lacking an explicit expression for saying: 'Yes, that's a new class that's forming.'

I'm going to draw on the example Norbert Elias gives us. It's not necessarily the right one, but it allows me to construct an extravagant parallel – and extravagance is my way of getting things moving and making them understood. Elias's great subject is to re-understand (rethink?) the civilizing process in bourgeois mode and no longer in the aristocratic manner, by questioning how the bourgeoisie came to occupy power and invent liberalism in opposition to the aristocracy and its values through the use of a whole series of models. So then, to sum up and paraphrase Elias, we could say: 'Just as the bourgeoisie scorned the limits of the aristocracy . . .' and make the following hypothesis, even if it's still just a hypothesis about the future: '. . . likewise we can imagine an ecological class that would direct a similar rebuke at the middle class: you have the same political limits, the same limits to your horizon for action as the aristocracy when the bourgeoisie was on the rise.'

Now there's an enormous gigantomachy for you, I have to admit! Still, all this allows us to understand a truly astonishing and important expression that Elias employs. He explains that at the time of its rise, the bourgeoisie was 'more rational' than the aristocracy because it imagined and endowed itself with a far vaster horizon for action than the aristocracy's, in particular through the discovery of production and the sudden development of its productive forces. That's something that can clearly be seen, moreover, in Proust, in that whole series of markers he uses. Elias's expression, about a more rational bourgeoisie,

seems to me extremely interesting. For in my phan-
tasmagoria, I contend that the ecological class needs
to say: 'We're more rational than you, the liberal
bourgeoisie, because for the whole of the 20th century, you couldn't be bothered understanding that
the fundamental situation into which production was
inserted was the planet's conditions of habitability,
and because you really stuffed those up. You are irra-
tional.' How can we begin to a imagine how a class
could talk about rationality after having ignored, for
a century, the issue of ecology, the issue of the temperature? Production is very important, of course.
The questions of how that production is distributed
are also important. But all of that remains slotted,
included, fitted into what enables it, and which *we*
consider as having priority. That's where we can, and
must, give the ecologists pride. Pride is very important.

We, the ecological class, say with pride: 'We're
the ones who represent the new rationality and the
new civilizing process, because we're tackling the
fundamental problem of the planet's conditions of
habitability.' That's a redefinition of the action horizon, a projection into the temporal horizon. And it's
definitely what's missing in today's politics, which is
why that's such a disaster. The liberal middle class
talks about economic recovery, but its heart isn't
in it, particularly since Covid: it's abandoned ship.
Well, it's very important for a class to have a horizon,
because, first of all, a class is a project. Today there's
no class yet to say: 'We are taking over now, we are
the temporal horizon.'

That horizon should not be understood in terms of
progress. It's complex: it's not progress but it *is* pros-

perity, all the same. Prosperity and progress aren't the same thing. It's not a matter of replaying old-style liberation, out of ignorance of the conditions of existence and abandonment of the past. It's about finding this other kind of liberation by recognizing: 'I'm discovering that I depend on all these lifeforms, whether they be bees, swallows, the climate . . . and it's good to depend.' That then poses an additional problem for political philosophy: reference to the notion of autonomy, to what it means to be autonomous, is very badly constructed. We need somehow to become 'heteronomous'! We can't move quickly on these matters, because we need to reinvent. And it's because we're changing cosmologies that it's so complicated. We need to find a political force that can work on these questions, a political force capable of saying: 'You're always complaining that there's no more fiction, no utopia, no sense to history . . .'

NT: No great narrative.

BL: Yes. '. . . but *we* have a great alternative narrative.' That's what socialism did: for fifty years, it created alternative narratives about history, evolution . . . People don't realize the enormous intellectual and cultural work done by economic scientists, first by the liberals, then by the socialists. Ecologists have the same work to carry out, meaning the work of redefining what history is, what science is – that's very important – and redefining the temporal horizon, which doesn't necessarily have to be that of progress, development, or going to Mars. What we need to define today is a politics whose definition of class struggle is evident in its ways of relating to the question: 'Are you maintaining the planet's conditions of habitability, which you have described precisely and from within which you can now distinguish what matters and what doesn't?' Those who ally themselves with the fundamental question of habitability would thereby be class brothers, brothers in struggle, as it were. And at that point we'd lapse back into classic politics where everyone fights about everything. But that's normal, and at least we'd know what to fight about. In the disaster that is today's politics, we don't know what to fight about.

You have to admit, it's a bit of a free-for-all: what horizon do we have? I'm 75 now and I remember that, right up till Mitterrand, we managed more or less to get our bearings in politics by looking at the parties, the programmes, or the slogans. It was possible to know what each one's interests were, and who to vote for. There was a possible alignment: 'I'm of my class, I have my interests, and parties and programmes to represent them, and I vote.' All that has disintegrated. The fact that the abstentionists are at 65% is not insignificant. We've changed worlds, and by force of circumstances, the corresponding parties have been completely pulverized, one after the other. The old alignment has ended up vanishing, and we're not going to be able to get it back by forming a party that aspires to occupy the Elysée. On that score, the ecologists are having themselves on. These days, we need to build from the bottom up. What interests me is working out how a civilized society manages to reconstitute itself on its own by reconstituting a definition of its own specific territory, meaning of its affiliations, and so of its interests, and so of its connections, its class associations . . . That's the way to set up shop. After that, there will be parties and, later, elections in which we can vote for the parties, but that's years down the track.

We find ourselves in this extraordinary situation where the alignment that for close to two centuries organized politics around the struggle between liberals and socialists is completely blown to smithereens. We can see numerous different reasons for this, notably the role of social networks. But I think in spite of everything that what weighs most heavily on all our political affects is this new climate regime to which no one gives a name, and which no one recognizes as the fundamental problem. The issue is no longer production and the distribution of wealth; it bears at present on what encompasses, encircles, what enables the system of production but is much more important than it is. At the end of the day, who am I to be able to put forward this proposal for another class? I'm no one, I just name . . . But the concept I name allows us to give ecologists heart, pride.

Inventing collective apparatuses

NT: Your method consists in putting apparatuses in place, notably within collectives; you work 'collectively'. Is that precisely linked to your conception of philosophy and sociology?

BL: In 2002, at the Karlsruhe Centre for Art and Media, ZKM, we put together the exhibition 'Iconoclash'. Not 'iconoclasm', the act of destruction, but 'iconoclash', the act of destruction suspended, uncertain.

It was an absolutely remarkable exhibition of ideas designed to deal with a question that I, myself, couldn't manage to resolve directly. There were seven different specialists there, in art history, Judaism, architecture, and science, since there's also a scientific iconoclasm in the notion of thinking without images. We'd constructed – this is what's so beautiful in the exhibition and that can't be done in a book – an immense, extraordinarily beautiful space. A space visitors passed through, asking themselves this eminently philosophical question: 'What does it mean to be a constructivist?' It was an absolutely weird collective and apparatus, going from Malevich to Catholic sanctuaries destroyed by Protestants and the other way round. There've been several theses on the exhibition since. All these collectives are also veritable detours, because I'm not capable of sorting out all these questions on my own.

NT: You often say you create collectives of people more expert than you.

BL: Yes. People who know more than I do.

NT: But you direct all the questions asked nevertheless.

BL: I ask a question because it's my job as a philosopher. I had, for instance, worked and written a lot on the Parliament of Things. But writing essays is the easy part. In posing the question: 'What would it mean to represent non-humans in an assembly? What could happen in an assembly where the lifeforms being talked about represented themselves?', the most sensational thing was setting up, with Frédérique Aït-Touati, just before COP 2015, an experiment involving loads of students and telling ourselves together that we were going to do it for real. Well, make-believe for real – that is, just by creating a situation. So then, in a theatre in Nanterre, several hundred students played at creating that situation, so as to test the aptness of a philosophical problem I'd posed. 'What happens at an Assembly when we have not only the United States, France, Germany, Brazil, but also a delegation from the Amazon – not Brazil, but the Amazon – or an ocean delegation, an Arctic delegation, an oil delegation, each of them speaking on their own behalf?' And as in the COPs, a committee secretary says: 'United States, you have two and a half minutes; Ocean, you have two and a half minutes.' And there follow the facts of detailed negotiations whereby the United States hears the Ocean's contribution on questions to do with the sea catches they were embarked on. It's fascinating! Of course, there's a certain naïvety in this process, which remains a fiction, a bit of role playing; but it allows us to deal with an absolutely fundamental philosophical problem and to make it heard anew.

These things we're talking about, that are captured by the ecological question, that get into politics and have always been part of the political question even though people still aren't aware of it – there really has to be a moment when all these things 'have a voice in the chapter'. So, there you have another way of presenting this idea, using a religious metaphor this time. What does it mean 'to have a voice in the chapter'? I did a whole book on that, *Politiques de la nature*.[1] It means constructing something in the nature of an Assembly. And it's utterly magnificent to be in a position to test it. Again in the same place, at the ZKM, we built a new exhibition that was just as fascinating from a philosophical point of view: 'Making Things Public'. Once more, the collectors we were talking about a moment ago were asked a fundamental question: how many ways are there right now of talking about non-humans, and how can we represent them simultaneously? Again, visitors crossing this immense space see things they would never have imagined. Negotiating, composing, assembling

---

[1] Published by La Découverte in 2004. Published in English as *Politics of Nature: How to Bring the Sciences into Democracy* (Harvard University Press, 2004); translated by Catherine Porter.

groups of citizens who decide the future – that's done in technology, in economics, in the law every bit as much as in Parliament. There was a Parliaments section in the exhibition, but it was just one small element, almost a stand, among all the other stands that represented collectors of other ways of talking politics. It was really beautiful doing it that way. The exhibition is a very beautiful and powerful medium, one that gives visitors the opportunity to deal with a philosophical problem through forms other than writing.

That's what I call empirical philosophy. Once more, it's collective: doing an exhibition means two hundred people working together for two years. I then learn an incredible number of things I didn't know. You could actually say that it's in the nature of a method, but in a way it's due to my limitations. I don't know how to deal with a question, so I get other people to deal with it: I put together in front of me groups of people who know a lot more about it than I do, to try to deal with questions that are fundamental but insoluble for me on my own when I'm sitting there trying to put essays together in my little office.

When Gaia intruded – to take up Isabelle Stengers's expression – I said to myself: 'This is too powerful. I'm going to be crushed by this face-to-face meeting with Gaia.' So once again I brought together people who knew more than I did, Frédérique Aït-Touati and Chloé Latour, and I said to them: 'It seems to me that theatre is a medium ideally suited to the emotion produced by the arrival of this creature. Without theatre, it's too powerful, and the terms an essay allows us to use are too feeble, because this shift in cosmology is just far too emotionally moving.' And so we created a theatre piece, and after that I did three theatre conferences. It's not that I want to see myself as a playwright, at all. But since philosophy isn't a metalanguage, it can resonate with other modes. Using different media, an exhibition fosters the work of philosophy every bit as much as a play or a lecture does.

Anyone who thinks an exhibition of thinking is an application of the ideas of Monsieur Latour laid out in a physical space would be completely mistaken. In reality, it's just that Monsieur Latour doesn't have a clue, but feels he ought to think something; he needs the work of others to pull it off, and it's from this work and visitors' reactions that he can discover what it is he's looking for. And that's what's so beautiful. When philosophy stops being this sort of pretension to a fundament, it can then acquire completely different tools. Writing books is all very well but there are heaps of other things we need to do on top of that. For instance, we need to teach, we need to invent schools. I've invented, not schools, but several teaching apparatuses. At Sciences Po, I invented the SPEAP, the school of the arts of politics, which has been around for the past ten years.

Why? Because you can't tackle all these ecological questions without the arts. If you don't have affects capable of absorbing the ecological situation, it's far too heavy. You just have a knotted stomach and the work is insurmountable. So we need to find links with various other methods. But it's very hard to convince a French university that doing a play is just as important as doing a manual of economics or sociology! There aren't nearly enough people working on this

question today. For me it was very important that the
university learn to stop being the university invented
by Humboldt in the 19th century. It's not a matter
of forming a vanguard and expecting the project to
trickle down to the common folk; on the contrary, we
have to let the university, let its research power, help
in a perfectly practical way people who being sub-
jected to this transformation of the soil and are trying
to understand where they are. For us to reverse the
direction of the university and for it to stop being the
vanguard of fundamental research, we need of course
to continue that fundamental research, which remains
extremely important, but to turn it round to serving
those who are impacted. 'Serving' doesn't mean: 'I'll
teach you something you didn't know.' Thanks to
the modern history we're emerging from, we actually don't know what it's like to be on this new Earth
we've been thrust into. So we need to do all we can
to find tools we can use to explore this new situation,
to prevent people from panicking, from being disoriented, and from just going on witnessing the current
political despair.

NT: So, you've created experimental groups, collectives, schools. Are you aware of also having 'created a
movement', a 'school of thought'?

BL: There's an ecosystem I've benefited from enormously, but that ecosystem is extremely complex and
extremely diverse. It's not a movement of disciples, in
any sense that would've been used to define the philosophy schools of the past. There are no 'Latourians'
the way there are Deleuzians or Foucauldians. And
that's a good thing because that isn't the aim at all.
The aim has always been to create collectives where

the disciplines and the different types of media are all on an equal footing. That's very important. A number of young researchers I work with and esteem claim the right to say: 'The transformation we need to bring about so as to go from modernizing to ecologizing, meaning from a modernization situation to a situation where we stick within the limits of Earth's habitability while preserving both prosperity and freedom, is a transformation of such scope that it requires us to marshal all the disciplines, and to work on all possible and imaginable subjects, in the universities, in the museums, in all the institutions.'

I've helped in this moment of transition, and I hope to be able to help further so as to provide us with the tools. I haven't yet created a movement, but I think there is a real model for today there: the model of working collectively in completely different disciplines, which don't have the same media but tackle the same questions. A model that, rather than hoping to do scientific papers that will get published in first-tier or second-tier journals before percolating through the broader public, does the opposite and turns directly to that public, who find themselves in a disarray at least equal to that of the researchers. It's a model that's absolutely essential.

The truth of the religious

NT: In *Jubiler ou les tourments de la parole religieuse*,[1] you write this:

> ... that is what he wants to talk about, that is what he can't actually seem to talk about: it's as though the cat had got his tongue; as though he was spoilt for choice when it comes to words; as though it was impossible to articulate; he can't actually seem to share what, for so long, he has held so dear to his heart; before his nearest and dearest, he is forced to cover up; he can only stutter; how can he own up to his friends, to his colleagues, his nephews, his students?[2]

'He' is Bruno Latour, he is you. I'm not about to ask you whether you believe or you don't believe – I know that from a personal as much as a philosophical point of view that's not how these things are put

---

[1] Published by Les Empêcheurs de penser en rond in 2002. Published in English as *Rejoicing, or the Torments of Religious Speech* (Polity, 2013); translated by Julie Rose.
[2] *Rejoicing*, p. 1.

– but will simply ask you: why is it so hard to speak religiously?

BL: Religious speech corresponds to a very peculiar type of veridiction: these are words that have the particularity of converting, of transforming those spoken to. Through their words and through what they say, Christians, preachers or believers, change the lives of the people they address. That's not what scientists seek to do in their laboratories, or politicians in their election campaigns, or lawyers in their work . . . The mode of veridiction employed by the religious is, to repeat, completely particular: its tonality and what we call its felicity conditions (meaning, it can fail) are specific to it. That's what's interesting in these different modes of veridiction: they can fail. You only have to go and listen to a sermon to see that in fact things do very often fail. I buried my poor sister a few days ago; the disastrous sermon given by the absolutely sinister priests at her funeral was a completely abortive speech act that converted absolutely no one in the church. Just as scientific facts are rarely discovered, so, too, religious utterance is rare.

But it turns out that this very curious form of speech, which changes the person spoken to, can also in some way be associated with the idea of absolute truth. The great German Egyptologist Jan Assmann, a man I really love, has written fascinating books on the issue. His idea is that what we call religion in our western culture corresponds in fact to a religion that introduces the notion of truth into religious questions. Well, till that point, a religion didn't have to be true. There was the religion of the Greeks, or even the religion of Athens, which was different from Sparta's.

Those religions were civil – and not just civil – forms that didn't require people to believe that it was the true religion. But what does 'true' mean? This is where the question of modes of veridiction is essential. The true in the sense of veridiction is the power to transform the person I'm addressing by what I say. It's precisely this truth mode of the conversion that has travelled from millennium to millennium through acts of charity, the acts that define what we can call faith.

And then there's a truth that says: 'Our God is the true God,' and thereby risks spilling over onto other forms of truth. Assmann reckons that's what happens with Judeao-Christianity. It's a complete novelty: no Greek would have said: 'Apollo is the true God,' or 'Zeus is the true God.' When this gobsmacking idea, that the notion of truth could be associated with the notion of God, enters the world, the true begins to eat into, to make a dent in, the other forms of truth. The religious then begins to invade the other modes while claiming not just to be true in its own specific mode, but also true in morality, true in science, true in law.

The passage you quoted deals with this total incomprehension of the religious, the most dire consequence of which is felt in the political. What I mean is that if religion is true beyond its own specific mode, then it has a hegemonic vocation to get involved in the political. The master of us all, the great Spinoza, introduces this essential issue in an extraordinary essay which he actually calls a 'theological-political' – the word is a bit strange – treatise, in a bid to try to unravel it in a different epoch: can we save the political? Can we save its specific mode of truth, save it from the religious, which also has its own mode of truth?

If I'm flagging the fact that this question was posed in the 17th century, that's because it's posed today: we, too, have a few theological-political problems, not just with the Christian religion, but with the other religions equally. To be able to undo this connection to the truth in the political sense, we need to extract the type of veridiction specific to the religious mode. It's fascinating; it requires us to go back to the age of Constantine and understand how things were playing out in several stages: back to the moment the Christian religion becomes an institution, and again to the 12th century, with the invention of what's known as Caesaropapism, meaning the idea that the Christian religion will thenceforth determine the general management of the administration, of civilization, that it will take charge of everything from the intimate morality of hearts and minds right up to general politics. There are other, later examples; every time what's lost is the soundness of the political mode and the soundness of the religious mode.

That term Spinoza uses might seem strange but it's extremely important: it's most definitely a theological-political question that's been posed throughout our entire history. The endeavour undertaken in that book [*Rejoicing*], as in heaps of other operations, was to salvage the originality proper to the religious so as not to confuse it either with faith, or with the idea that it's a means of ordering the world, of taking charge of morality, taking charge of politics.

NT: And yet when we read you, we get the impression that if theology can't come to the rescue of politics, it can nevertheless try to take care of the issue of ecology. I'm thinking notably of *Laudato si'*, the pope's encyclical letter of 2015, which voices the cry of the Earth and the cry of the poor. On the one hand, the theological, especially in these cyclical times, appears to be up to the job of taking care of the climate question and helping us get over our bewildering impotence in the face of the crisis. On the other, you agree with Jan Assmann that the monotheistic expression of theology, which seeks both to separate nature and culture and to show the hegemony of its mode of existence at the same time, has in a way committed the sin of the Moderns. How can we work through this paradox?

BL: This business of the spiritual has been stuck in a rut for a good three centuries now; science's hegemony grab corresponds to such a shift in religious hegemony that all that's left to the unhappy religious is to talk about the supernatural. For theologians, the ecology moment has indubitably had the effect of reopening a space and an obligation to engage in interpretation. That's what I say to them: 'Look at the fabulous chance you've got. For one and a half centuries you've been wondering if you needed to modernize the Church, and now you don't have to ask yourself that question any more: the modernity you fought against, in which you didn't know how to place yourself, is no longer the problem. Modernity is ending right in front of you.' But in spite of everything, they still can't agree. It's still incredibly hard to explain to bishops or priests that ecology is an immense opportunity to revisit, for instance, the question of the Incarnation. And yet this idea, now abandoned, according to which the world is at issue before heaven, is a tradition of the Church itself, a classic question once crucial to the Church Fathers.

The end of modernity allows the Church once again to open up this field of reflection and to rediscover its own tradition, of a God made man. Of a God who is in the Earth, who is in creation, who is part of that creation, who is a co-witness, in the same state of flux as that creation. With ecology, an opportunity opens up in relation to theology: there are heaps of inventions to make, which might get people to stop talking about the Virgin Mary or loads of other things that are all so many successive screens that have piled up. Every one of those screens was invented for good reasons, but those reasons now go back several centuries.

You're right to cite that phrase linking the cry of the poor and the cry of Gaia. It obviously makes no sense from the viewpoint of the Moderns' cosmology: the Earth doesn't cry and no one hears the poor when they do, either. This extraordinary fusion is impossible to imagine in a secular world, where 'poor' signifies 'socially underprivileged', and where 'a poor soul' as theology understands it is meaningless. But with ecology we're going to be able to seize on altogether new possibilities. What the pope does so magnificently is to invent a new myth. And a lot of people, a lot of priests and cardinals, are furious about this stunning invention: 'our Sister, Mother Earth'.[3] It's so bizarre! How to interpret it? What is a priest supposed to do

---

[3] 'Encyclical Letter *Laudato si'* of the Holy Father Francis on Care for Our Common Home' (24 May 2015).

when the pope says something like that? From then on, the opportunity is open.

We mustn't see ecology as the new religious ideology; we need to see it in its capacity to open up a possibility. That's a very broad version of ecology that allows there to be an accord between us, not necessarily all Christians, but all of us who are witnessing the end of modernity and who are trying to understand how we can get back to the values of the political. It's actually an opportunity to re-civilize ourselves. We were civilized with modernity, but badly, since we've come to this impasse. We can now re-civilize ourselves through the issue of ecology.

Science in action

NT: Unlike many other thinkers dealing with living things today, you didn't come to ecology via the defence of endangered species or spaces. What are the issues, of sociology and the philosophy of the sciences, that brought you to it?

BL: Ecology isn't my main subject. I came to it through analysis of the activity of scientists, an area I fell into when I started observing *science in action* – that's the title of a collection of essays I published many years ago with Michel Callon,[1] about science 'as it is done', and not 'done (and dusted)' science. Science is always done controversially, meaning, in mixes of little bits of politics, little bits of ego, the simple little dynamics of competition between scientists. Currently, this is perfectly observable in the science of Covid, or of pesticides, or in the science relating to climate issues, for instance.

[1] *Science in Action: How to Follow Scientists and Engineers Through Society* (Harvard University Press, 1987).

And science is also done in a few very precise places, rare sites. I want to talk about this laboratory object, which has fascinated me for fifty years. It's there that facts and discoveries are established, ones as important and interesting as endorphin, for instance. Everyone knows about endorphin now! But in studying this laboratory space, at the Salk Institute in San Diego, day after day I saw endorphin being made, emerging so to speak from this artificial place I was in. That's what fascinated me. You arrive full of the classic epistemology of Science with a capital S, but in practice you notice this absolutely wonderful thing: it's because the laboratory is artificial that it can establish solid facts. It's because they're rare places, that you arrive at certainties. A discovery is a very rare thing.

NT: Why did you, as a sociologist, get interested in the sciences and in laboratories?

BL: Laboratories allow you to consider this fabulous contradiction, that objectivity is something produced, manufactured. That's a gigantic philosophical problem, which epistemology has been dealing with for three hundred years: how do we arrive at scientific truth – that is, how can we link, in the same sentence, 'It's manufactured' and 'It's true'? And how do we deal with that question? I answer: 'Let's go and see.' That detour has become my usual method for dealing with problems. To answer a philosophical question as passive as that, you need a field, you need a place. A place where you can see how it's done, how it's manufactured. That's the way Michel Foucault proceeded.

And it's for that precise reason that I spent two years in a laboratory: to tackle a philosophical question, only through the detail of an analysis of practices. There, I realized that this great mystery is entirely studiable empirically by retracing how, in a few hours, we go from 'It's some sort of endorphin, but it's not yet quite certain' to 'It's solid, it's an established fact.' An insoluble philosophical problem – how do we arrive at scientific truth? – becomes empirically studiable. And only an empirical study allows that; it's what makes field studies so exciting. Obviously, to understand how it happens, you have to spend some time there and combine a whole series of principles, methods, anthropology, philosophy, to be able to analyse some amazing things. It's absolutely sensational that endorphin is still only a probability at five in the afternoon and then, at five-thirty, it's a fact.

NT: Yes, indeed. So how is it possible?

BL: Well, it all happens using tools that are minuscule, but that are the culmination of what takes place in the laboratory. This goes from, say, the way the laboratory rats react to a question applied to them, like what you're actually seeing when you inject them with an endorphin, to the answer that colleagues are going to come back with, contradicting the initial hypotheses, over and over again. These are series of controversies that can't be short-circuited, because it's controversy that allows us to qualify the answer produced by the laboratory, or to make it a lot surer, a lot firmer. The one I studied was a collegial environment where people criticized what was in the process of happening with endorphin. But you have to take into account that there were four or five other laboratories in competition at the same time, and that from one laboratory to the next, even the name 'endorphin' could be different. You get to a moment of stabilization where uncertainty disappears. It's an incredible thing: you see that the facts are 'fabricated', but that they're sure. It's got absolutely nothing to do with some scientific method, because it's all done haphazardly! That's what I show in detail: you look for different resources in the laboratory to get to the point of stabilizing this famous object that concentrates everyone's attention.

That's how this thing magnificently described by Isabelle Stengers happens: the idea that this endorphin, which is still only an inchoative fact, authorizes you to speak on its behalf to say what it is. At that particular moment, your subjective production, the fact that you have colleagues and that there's a company behind you – all that disappears: at that instant, the established fact speaks in a way for itself. For itself, in an artificially built laboratory with a whole social world behind it so as to authorize the endorphin to speak, of course. That particular object was so beautiful it had completely eluded the philosophy of the sciences, which considered, on the contrary, that science was precisely what removed you from opinion, what no longer had anything whatsoever to do with the social or the political. I spent two years in my laboratory seeing exactly the opposite. Opinion, the social, the political, are precisely the practices scientists throw themselves into, those that allow them to produce objective facts. My colleagues and I have been working for forty-five years to prove that particular obvious fact; together we've created a veritable history of the sciences, a sociology of the sciences. But, in my view, not a single drop of this has percolated through to the scientists.

NT: How come?

BL: It's a question of hegemony; that's the right term, I think. It can't be said our area of research has had a huge impact, so heavily does the hegemony of Science with a capital S weigh on every analysis of society – French society in particular, but not only.

NT: As in the current health crisis.

BL: This crisis clearly shows the way scientists are asked to immediately produce facts. 'You're scientists, so you produce facts.' But that's just not true! Which is what Isabelle Stengers never stops showing in her own way. Facts are rare; it's very rare for there to be scientific discoveries. The idea of an all-purpose scientific method, where all that's needed is to slip into a white lab coat for any utterance at all to be considered Science with a capital S – it's a lie. It's a deception, because what works for one discipline is not going to work for another. Even within a discipline, what succeeds in one case is not necessarily going to function for the following case. So, the idea my colleagues and I had was to take the sciences off-site again – these sciences that supposedly derive from 'the view from nowhere', to borrow Donna Haraway's phrase[2] – and back to the network in which they're produced. We immediately caused a real stir: hyperventilating philosophers called it an attack on science! On the contrary: it was an attack on epistemology, not on the sciences or scientific practices. I maintain today that the sciences are better understood and better defended when they're recognized as humble scientific

[2] See Thomas Nagel, *The View from Nowhere* (Oxford University Press, 1986).

practices that don't have the aim of constructing a view of the universe 'from nowhere' – and I have to say, for me, the climate crisis and the Covid crisis are further proof of that.

If the practice of science arrives at objective facts – the only ones we can be scientifically certain of – that's precisely because it's done among different colleagues and followed in detail, precisely because it builds artificial laboratories and it has to be financed, precisely because it makes mistakes, it hesitates, and it's rare. But this didn't make it into the doxa, into the everyday doctrine, of scientists.

NT: Things are starting to change, notably with the Intergovernmental Panel on Climate Change (IPCC). You relate that certain members of the IPCC sometimes tell you they need you and your philosophy of the sciences to understand what's happening to us.

BL: The climate sciences are particularly interesting: they're made up of physics, chemistry, numerous models and algorithms, and they depend at the same time on buoys in the ocean, satellites, core samples . . . In short, it's a puzzle with hundreds of millions of different pieces of data. Not a hypothetical-deductive science, as past philosophers reckoned. It's a science that puts together multiple pieces of data, so it's as solid as a carpet woven with a thousand strands. With this same puzzle, it was established, practically from the early '80s, that CO_2 would drive up the temperature of the planet. Because people were quite certain about that, those who were working on the climate thought that action would follow. They were in for a shock. Not only did action not follow, but on top of that they got attacked at the very point where they thought they'd be able to defend themselves with the authority of science: 'The science says that . . .' All the countless lobby groups immediately countered that it was all *fake news* and that the science was saying something else entirely. I've done a lot of work on this brawl, which took off in the '90s and isn't finished yet.

What interested me especially is that it allowed scientists – climate scientists, Earth system scientists, critical zone scientists – to realize that they were very badly defended by the famous epistemology that sticks a capital S on science, and which they relied on to be able to say 'The science says that; action will follow.' Science says that, but action doesn't follow, because obviously Science with a capital S doesn't exist. They were in way defending themselves with a wooden sword by saying: 'Look, we're scientists, we're right.' They got themselves attacked; it was demoralizing. That was the moment some of them came to see us, my colleagues in the sciences and me, to ask for our help. But the condition for our help was that they would have to accept the idea of being a practice, situated within very particular and very costly networks, a practice that needs to be sustained with great attention. We have to rid ourselves of the false and all-purpose idea that from the moment someone's a scientist, what they say is scientific. Scientists aren't universal; science doesn't function on its own.

The problem is that scientists want to have their cake and eat it: they want both the scientific practice and the hegemony of their particular way of defining the truth over the others, which are opinion, morality, religion . . . And so, even economists say they're scientists, when that is strictly meaningless. The word 'scientist' is used like a rallying cry. It's a way of grabbing a javelin to attack, but it has absolutely nothing to do with the practice of science.

The modes of existence

NT: In *Enquête sur les modes d'existence*, that great book that appeared in 2012, published by La Découverte, your main publisher, you oppose the hegemony of science, religion, and certain other modes of existence. Is philosophy, in your view, actually the guardian of the plurality of modes of existence?

BL: I never know if I'm a sociologist or a philosopher . . .

NT: Well, then, that's the question to ask!

BL: At bottom, I'm a philosopher, but one who also tries to resolve a sociological question: the question of knowing what society is made of. It's assumed to be made of social relations. But in a work, once again collective, that I had the chance to do with friends at the Centre de sociologie de l'innovation (CSI) in the École des Mines, we argued that sociology is not the science of the social, but the science of associations. Sociology looks at heterogeneous associations between things that have nothing to do with each other: bits of technology, bits of law, bits of the sciences . . .

I've always thought there was a genuine philosophical question behind all of that. My colleagues, who are proper sociologists, never agreed with me. For a classical philosopher like me, the question is a question about truth. What is truth? It's in philosophy's DNA, if we can use that vulgar expression, to be interested in the totality. It might be a matter of a Hegelian totality, but there are many other totalities, too, like Whitehead's, for instance.

NT: Meaning that philosophy tries to think about the whole.

BL: It tries to think about the whole, and all that the world is made of. It's a banal question, but one I've always considered absolutely obvious. And, at the same time, philosophy as it is just can't manage to do that, and it knows it can't. It's not necessarily negative, but it's in the dark, it's feeling its way. I refer back to my absolutely classic philosophy question: what is truth?

Working on the question of truth in its religious mode of existence already gave me a certain idea about it. I also got interested in the production of objectivity within the framework of my laboratory study. And within that framework, we're definitely dealing with a mode of truth; but the most amazing discovery was to see to what extent it's local. If you miss a single step on the complex path that takes you from the laboratory, where they test rats, to publication, the facts evaporate. You can only get to the truth by going from point to point. I don't know why, but ever since I was a child this question of the point to point – meaning, the fact of 'going through' – has always interested me. You can't skip steps and you have to pay the price for every step you go through.

It might seem strange to attribute this question of the point to point to the great questions of philosophy. But that's my method, if you can call it a method: taking an interest in the question of the whole, but getting to the whole through a very meticulous mechanism that isn't direct. It's only step by step that you gain objectivity in a laboratory. In a court, you also have to go from point to point without missing a single step: it allows you to get yourself organized. That's the reason I got so interested in the law. The 'legally true' is a stunningly beautiful example of what an alternative, completely different truth can be. If you say: 'I'm sorry, you may well be right, but legally you're in the wrong,' anyone will understand what that means. You also understand when a barrister acknowledges your testimony, your trauma, but informs you that, legally, you're at fault. If it's the judge who says that, the case is closed. There's a type of truth absolutely specific to the law that everyone understands as being separate, but also sound, or 'legally sound', to be more specific. The adverb 'legally' is respected as a mode of existence, a mode of truth that's separate and doesn't spill over, or slobber, so to speak – meaning, it doesn't have any particular hegemony over the others.

When I arrived at the CSI, I'd been thinking for a long while about setting modes of truth alongside each other and comparing them. That's how the question of truth, and the parallel sociological question of what our society is made of, are linked. Our society is made of law, science, technology, religion – made of all these different regimes and modes of truth. It's these associations of bits and pieces that compose society: the social is made of all these segments, of different types of truths that are incompatible with each other.

When you say to someone: 'I'm sorry, you've been through an appalling trauma, but it's legally inadmissible,' that doesn't appease them, but they recognize a technical mode of truth that's very particular, specific to the judicial. In other words, this mode of truth is separate from the others, it has its own power, its own pride and its own competence, which are completely different from those of the sciences. We don't say: 'Legally that's true, but it's also true scientifically.' At least not that way round, because, conversely, scientists don't hesitate to say that what is scientifically true is consequently true across the board for the whole set of things, and that the others, members of religious orders, lawyers, politicians, produce nothing more than opinions. The invention of physics, of chemistry, of biology, are discoveries of extraordinary beauty, but in the modern moment, the scientific mode of truth was set up in such a way that all those sciences were crammed together in an across-the-board epistemology and carted into the stratosphere, in a view from nowhere. In those days, the other practices were told that their methods, their objects of thought, their results and discoveries, were nothing but subjectivity – that the world was already made. Such a thing constitutes a crime; you completely annihilate both the different modes of truth, which you squash at the same time, and the truth of the scientific mode itself – you don't say how it's constructed, or how you arrive at these things, and you lose the point-to-point process of scientific production.

If the law serves me, after a fashion, as a compass, that's because it isn't necessarily domineering. Of course, there's been the odd bid for hegemony on its part, but we wouldn't be happy to hear it said that all the other modes are legal modes, probably because the law is so old – much older than the sciences – that it's already constituted within a constellation of several modes of truth established alongside each other. To answer your initial question, this is where philosophy changes course in my view. It pursues its enterprise of research and of questioning the truth, but it accepts the probability of finding several versions of this; not in a relativist sense where there is no truth, but in the sense in which each mode defines a way of telling the truth that's different from the next.

It's crucial to work through these questions if we're interested in the political. Because people completely forget there is a truth when it comes to politics. Politicians are scorned as people, accused of talking rubbish, of indulging in rhetoric, in the most banal sense of the term. But it's precisely because of the scorn directed at politics that there are so few studies about lying or telling the truth in politics. Well, there certainly is a truth in politics: everyone knows perfectly well how to distinguish the falseness or truth of what's being said, the authenticity or inauthenticity of words used, and every political personality knows perfectly well deep down when they're lying or not. Even if it remains very hard to dredge up, there is one totally clear criterion: in the long circle that goes from the inarticulate complaint to the order given by some authority, do your words allow you to go from one step to the next and to construct the circle in such a way that it turns? If you fix things so the circle doesn't turn, then you're lying. You're lying politically, for once again we're dealing here not with a scientific, legal, or religious lie, but with a political lie. The question of respect for the political has always interested me. To make the political respectable, we have to go via its mode of truth so as to analyse it and understand it in its own right.

Apart from the law, politics, the sciences, I've also spent a lot of time working on another extraordinarily beautiful mode: technology. Technical truth is very different from the others, and far more problematic. It poses the question of knowing whether a thing is well or badly constructed, for example.

NT: 'Does it work?'

BL: 'Does it work? Is it technically good?' We musn't confuse sciences and technologies, because they're two different modes of existence. If a thing is technically good, that doesn't mean it will be scientifically right. Many historians of technology have shown this: engineers sail through scientific taboos with cheery indifference! They charge ahead because scientific truth is not their problem. Their question is a question of technical truth.

There's a whole literature of accumulated philosophical guff on the issue of technology and the advent of the technological reign. Yet every machine we use is but a moment, a freeze-frame, in a project of continual transformation that mobilizes a series of completely heterogeneous resources. Technology is overrun by the legal, for instance! To grasp this, you only have to picture the hundreds of lawyers who gathered together to calibrate the codes and standards for telecommunications devices, or for any other machine we use. If we want to think about the technical, we need to look at it within this constant movement, meaning in relation to the issue of the project rather than of the technical object.

Similarly, this movement of transformation traverses and in part composes the famous collective, the nature of which we're trying to understand. It's not the social collective imagined by classical sociology, which immediately imagines a form of superstructure in which all social relations would hold together. That's like butter; it has no solidity! There's no collector in such a sociology; we don't know how these famous collective phenomena that nonetheless obsess sociologists are collected. Being interested in the collective without the collector is like being interested in garbage bins without ever asking ourselves about garbage collectors! So that's precisely the question that interests us, my colleagues and me: what is this collector?

Once sociology presents itself as the science of associations, things start to take shape and hold together. You begin by positing that the collective is collected by scientists, by politicians, by lawyers, by technologists, and as you study, say, the associations between law and technology, the collective takes on meaning and substance.

The reason I never know whether I'm a sociologist or a philosopher is that I'm interested in modes of existence so as to be able to understand the social.

And that's also the reason I'm really a philosopher after all – I can't understand the social if I'm not a philosopher capable of thinking about modes of existence.

The circle of politics

NT: In your view, 'militants' borrow their relationship to the absolute, and to the absolute truth, from religion, even if they declare themselves to be profoundly anti-religious. They lay claim to the true politics, and present themselves as the bearers of political truth. And so you prefer the attitude of 'activists'. What distinction do you make between a militant and an activist, and how do you link that with the question of political truth?

BL: To think about politics, obviously you don't make do with parties and elections; you have to get away a bit from the official world of politics and simply go back to the problem of the collective. In the sociology of association, a collective is something that has to be produced. There has to be a collector to collect it, because phenomena aren't in themselves collective. I've already referred to technical, religious, scientific collectors ... But what's quite rightly known as 'speaking with one voice', based on a multiplicity of people who have completely different ideas and

84

positions, is also a very important form of political collector.

It requires an extraordinary metamorphosis to reach a situation where one person can say: 'I'm speaking on your behalf,' and another person can reply: 'Yes, if I myself were speaking, I'd say exactly the same thing you're saying.' Likewise in a situation where someone receives an order given by someone else and says: 'If it was my turn to speak, I'd say the same thing.'

How is this very particular mode produced, ensuring as it does that when a single person speaks, a hundred, a thousand, ten thousand, or ten million people say: 'Yes, that's exactly what I think'? It's not just the fact that what I say is identical to what the other person's saying. It's not some 'same' thing that's being said, but once again an absolutely point-by-point transformation, from one to the other. This way of functioning is familiar to us; we encounter it in all places in society where individuals embody a collective voice. It might be a director, or a producer ... Any person who has employees is obliged to do politics all the time. The father of a family or the mother of a family has the same obligation to form a collective, since there's no one and nothing else to do the job. It's not easy to hold together; a collective will constantly scatter because the things people say end up being completely transformed. If, for instance, you make a complaint, that complaint may well give rise to a whole host of successive metamorphoses, translations into an order or a suggestion given, or a regulation if we're now talking more official frameworks. Whatever the framework, you always have to imagine yet again, point by point, that what you're going to say will be the same thing, but expect that it will be completely transformed, point by point.

It's by accepting that I speak in a certain way, so that what I say can move on to the next person in the chain of transformation, and by being aware that it will be turned into something completely different in the process, that we discover a criterion of truth or falseness. That's a simplified scenography of things, but all the way along the political circle that goes from the inarticulate complaint to the order given, this difference between what I say and what is said must be maintained. If there's no resemblance, politics ebbs away. It's here, too, that the truth criterion is most often lacking. It's a delicate business. Imagine a society of sixty million French people, in which a complaint turns into a grievance, then a regulation, and finally comes back in the form of an order given – there probably won't be any relationship of resemblance between the original utterance and the utterance that comes back. Now imagine that the sixty million French people lose this capacity to produce politics and say: 'I take no notice of the issue of politics. I stick to my values, I stick to my opinion.' Sticking to your opinion comes down to lying politically, because by definition an opinion should be transformed so it can move on to the next person, who will have a different definition of things, which they in their turn will pass on until it finally comes back to you.

This mode of truth is incredibly precarious: it can collapse any second! Any company manager, any father, any mother, any head of state, knows it's impossible to achieve this continual transformation without betrayal. Well, that betrayal is necessary. To go back to the distinction you mentioned, that's precisely what militants don't get. Militants aren't content with borrowing the mode of truth of the religious; they import a completely secularized version of it, stripped of its movements of mutation, transformation, exegesis, mediation.

The militant has completely lost all these gestures involved in defining the political. Unlike someone who knows that on an issue about wind turbines at a certain spot, or an issue about migrants at another, it will take a colossal amount of work to arrive at the point where it all returns in the form of regulations or orders given and for those orders finally to be obeyed and followed – that's what I call an activist. And the frightening requirement of politics, what's so terrible about it, is that it demands that this colossal amount of work be started all over again – because if you stop the movement, everyone will scatter again like sparrows.

NT: Can you give us an example of what you call this necessary betrayal?

BL: The fundamental betrayal that recurs most often resides in saying: 'I gave an order. That order will be obeyed.' How do you expect an order to be obeyed? The order you give will end up transformed. Nobody obeys an order; at best, people obey their own way of understanding what's been said. Once again, I'm staging things crudely, but when the people down at the bottom say: 'Myself, I think that, I've got my opinion, I've got my values and I'm sticking to them,' the situation gets complicated. If you stick to your values and your opinion, you're not doing politics, you're not preparing the next stage of the process. That's the first political mistake. The second mistake is to say: 'But I gave orders, I've already organized everything required. See, we've already done plenty of things. We've got plenty of regulations in place,' and to believe that will be obeyed. The first of these mistakes, believing in your opinions, sticking to them, and wanting them to be faithfully represented, in transparent and absolute fashion, is a recent form of catastrophe. If you demand an exact and correct representation, then you transfer into politics what I call the double-click, and politics disappears.

NT: This double-click concept is really interesting. It passes itself off as practically the personification of a certain attitude of mind by indicating, through an icon, an operation, that all computer users understand, the fact of short-circuiting mediation, of skipping a point.

BL: The double-click is a modern form of Satan! It's the idea that we can do without mediation. We find double-clicks in religion, among the fundamentalists. In politics, with the people who are militants rather than activists. We come across it again obviously in science in the notion that science gets done no matter where, and that as long as there's a white lab coat, there is science. Right now, partly because of the digital and online social networks, the ideal of all communication seems to have become this flow that goes from one 'myself, I think that' to the next, without any transformation being necessary; a sort of fundamental battle between political, scientific, or religious double-clicking that is now in reality destroying or shredding all modes, one after the other.

This is what we've largely been able to observe from the beginning of the Covid crisis: when scientists are confronted with a double-click, they find themselves accused of lying. Why? Fact production is incredibly slow and the quantity of information necessary to obtain those facts is enormous, and so scientists rightly say that they need time, statistics, instruments, and that they can't rush discovery of the facts. At the present moment, we're in a painful period where the accusation of lying is bandied about over the place. Fake news is a symptom of this. It's not that a section of people have suddenly gone mad, it's that the notion of mediation has disappeared. We're going through a general process of stamping out mediations that falsifies all the modes we need in order to live. We're right in the middle of a crisis of civilization in which everything that ensures our survival is being attacked through double-clicks. In the face of the *trouble-click*, any mode at all is untruthful. People don't realize that the real lie is the one offered by politicians who try to immediately satisfy the demands they're presented with: 'Are you transparent? Are you transferring my opinion, my suffering, without mediation?' Anyone elected would be obliged to say in all honesty: 'No, I can't. That will inevitably be transformed in some other committee. There's a whole arc of steps to be taken before things come back to us.'

NT: You write: 'How strange it is in the end. On the one hand, we get the impression that everything has played out, everything's lost, it's all over. On the other, that nothing's really begun.' Do you think that at the same time about philosophy, and politics, and religion, too?

The circle of politics

BL: We're living through a catastrophe which has turned today into a veritable tragedy because of our inability to react to it. We need to admit that we feel crushed by the situation. Well, even if it's obviously strange to say so, having presented the gravity of the moments we're going through in the switch from one mode of cosmology to another, I still think we're living in a fantastic time. Once again, we might draw a parallel with the 16th, 17th, and 18th centuries, which saw a similar upheaval as they moved from the old cosmologies to the cosmology of the Moderns. That was an incredibly beautiful time, too, lots of interesting things were happening in the arts, the sciences – in the whole culture! We find ourselves in a similar situation: things are opening up in front of us in an extraordinary way. In any case, I don't believe it's the role of a philosopher to add to the countless tears shed by the collapsologists and the catastrophists, but on the contrary to work at restoring agency.

I think ecology has been through a whole host of beliefs that we used to have when we were modern and which skewed it for a long time. Let's not forget that this business of modernity – of taking ourselves off to an uninhabitable world, a purely utopic, airborne world, a world where we were going to abandon everything to do with the beliefs of the past – is magnificently symbolized by the idea of a trip to Mars. Earth isn't exciting, but going to Mars – now, that's really something! It's fabulous that this sort of mythology of blast-off and flight is finally being ridiculed, that it's disintegrating, it's disappearing. To be perfectly honest, what a relief it is to come down to earth from that – even if in an enormous crash!

Because at least we're finally here. We're home, we can and we want now to try to understand what's happening. A landscape, a land, a new land, is now opening up at our feet, before our very eyes.

And on a new land, what do you need if not peoples? It's interesting to go back to the question 'What people on what land?' That's what I call, a bit surprisingly, 'the revival of ethnogenesis'. We don't realize to what extent modernity made it impossible for us to study whatever situation you care to mention. It was terrible being modern, being endlessly paralysed like that by the weight of the modernization front and the perpetual obligation to discriminate between what was modern and what was archaic. It was crippling to have to always shut everything down. Modernity shut us down. At present, all that has been swept aside, questions are opening up again. Obviously it's difficult and distressing . . . but what a relief!

Philosophy is so beautiful!

NT: When you're asked the question 'What is sociology?,' you answer: 'Sociology is not the science of the social; it's the science of associations.' But what do you say to the question 'What is philosophy?,' a question Gilles Deleuze and Félix Guattari notably tried to answer at the end of their collaboration? At the beginning of their book,[1] they say you can only ask that question late in the day, when old age has come upon you and it's time to speak concretely. They write:

> It was asked before ... but ... those who asked the question ... were not sober enough. There was too much desire to *do* philosophy to wonder what it was, except as a stylistic exercise. That point of nonstyle where one can finally say, 'What is it I've been doing all my life?' had not been reached.[2]

---

[1] *Qu-est-ce que la philosophie?* (Minuit, 1991). Published in English as *What is Philosophy?* (Columbia University Press, 1994); translated by Hugh Tomlinson and Graham Burchell.

[2] *What is Philosophy?*, p. 1.

What have you been doing all your life, Bruno, and
what is philosophy?

BL: The book by Gilles Deleuze and Félix Guattari is
very important. It's a beautiful book that sets out to
define the scientific modes, and also spends a lot of
time working on that other mode, which is the mode
of fiction. In fiction, too, you come across the question of truth, meaning that, amazingly enough, we
identify truth in it and so are able to acknowledge:
'Yes, that's true, fictionally.' It's a mode of existence
and of truth that's extraordinarily powerful.

NT: Can you give us an example of something true in
fiction, in literature?

BL: There's a lot of talk at the moment about Lucien
de Rubempré. Lucien de Rubempré exists as much as
this chair I'm sitting on.

NT: How can a character invented by Balzac in *Lost
Illusions* have such a solid existence?

BL: He's stayed the distance, so he has an incontestable
capacity to exist. Another philosopher, one Deleuze
read a lot and used as it happens, Étienne Souriau,
says magnificently that fictional characters have their
own proper mode, a mode that's all theirs. We can
say simultaneously that Rubempré exists and ask
ourselves: 'In what way does he exist? What's his
ontology?' You need to do speculative philosophy for
a second; philosophy has made the question of being
as a being its obsession. There is that which endures,
there is the flow of existence, but beyond that there's
something else in being that doesn't change. This is
an idea you find in religion as well as in philosophy,
and obviously in the sciences, wherever people tie
things that pass to laws of Nature which themselves

don't pass. It's a kind of obsession with the Moderns, this seeking to link the question of existence back to things that are more enduring than it is.

But we've changed cosmologies and now we're not just in the world of the living, but in the world of things that endure because they don't endure. All these modes of existence and truth have the particularity of being propped up by others; it's a way of opposing 'being as a being' that I call 'being as other'. For a being to continue existing, it must go through something other every time, just as on a completely mundane level I had to have my breakfast to come in here and talk to you. I'm continually swallowing a bit of the other to endure in my existence right to the end. There isn't a single being that doesn't have this particular quality: beings can't endure over time if they don't go through others. The idea of basing philosophy and an understanding of the world on what endures makes no sense, since all that endures does so precisely through what doesn't endure.

To close this speculative parenthesis and return to the question of modes of existence, what's interesting is to pinpoint every time the type of otherness that is used. In the case of fiction, when Balzac invents his character Lucien de Rubempré, he constantly asks himself whether he'll hold together. This holding together of the invented being doesn't amount to much more than a lot of paper covered in ink. But with that paper covered in ink – after a lot of coffee, a few lamb chops, and seventy-five oysters – Balzac produces a being who holds together on his own, if we hold him together ourselves for the time it takes to read Balzac's work. If we stop reading Balzac, obviously Rubempré disappears. We hold together, then, a very particular, very specific being, invented starting from scrawl. He holds up, and does so with an extraordinary force that grips you when you read that book. And yet he depends entirely on those who carry him on their shoulders, just as 'the Gauls were raised on a shield' – that metaphor of Souriau's is wonderful! This means that if you stop raising your Lucien de Rubempré, or if he's no longer taught in school, then he disappears.

This is also a problem in constructivism, with this whole question of beings who depend completely on their mode of production but who are nonetheless true. Every one of these beings offers a different definition of the constructed, of the well constructed, of what works and what doesn't. Every time we go to the cinema or see a play, we gauge whether the story and the characters stack up or not. Because if they don't, it's failed, and all you've spent or used is pointless! People who make films, or write or edit books, ask themselves these same questions. They're specific, because fiction doesn't depend on knowing whether Lucien de Rubempré really was born in this place or that – that wouldn't make any sense. It's more about a way of defining things that's peculiar to fiction, which offers a new understanding of otherness every time. It's a truth principle that's extraordinarily powerful. It's not scientifically sound, quite simply because the 'scientifically sound' is just one mode of truth production among others, alongside the ways fiction, politics, religion, and technology respectively produce truth in their own modes.

But let's get back to your general question, 'What is philosophy?' If I have to answer, as an old man at the end of his career, or following your beautiful quote, I'd say that it's not a metalanguage. It's not what will define being as a being. It's not what will define the foundation or underpinnings of all the rest, or what each thing is made of. Philosophy is a modest practice, one that also itself depends on scrawl. But it *is* indispensable. Philosophy really grabbed me from my very first lesson in my final year of high school. I said: 'I'm a philosopher,' because I felt like I just couldn't do without it. It manages to maintain – operationally, because I'm an empirical philosopher – the diverse modes of existence alongside each other. It allows us to get our bearings between the modes, at the very places where they try to colonize each other, in what I call category errors. These category errors are innumerable, and fascinating to observe and study: the scientist who says: 'Because I'm a nice guy and I've got a white lab coat, everything I say is scientific' is one example. He commits a category error by presenting himself as the mouthpiece of science and scientific truth, whereas in actual fact he doesn't have the laboratory, or the colleagues, or the tiniest piece of the confected apparatus that allows someone to speak on their behalf.

That, for me, is what philosophy is. First of all, it's necessarily collective. It's the fact of turning up, along with others, to pinpoint how the different modes can be maintained; the fact of managing to respect each other without trying to gobble each other up. It's essential to the relations between politics, religion, and science. We couldn't go on without acquiring criteria of distinction so that the different modes don't come and slobber over each other. Philosophy is very important, vital in the moment we're going through, because it's the thing that will allow us to stop the various modes destroying one another. This criterion of distinction must necessarily be studied empirically. The role of the philosopher is not to judge but to maintain subtle little processes for spotting category errors and to say: 'Is what you're saying there politically true?,' or to contradict someone who says: 'But there is no truth in politics, I do whatever I like, myself, what counts is winning,' by answering: 'No. There is a political truth and we need to be able to respect it.' It plays the same role in science, when scientists start to say that from the moment they're scientists, they can go anywhere.

It's not unrelated to Kant's three critiques, except that Kant sets himself up as a justice of the peace: that is, he comes up with a solution to the whole business. I think such a position is impossible today; philosophy is not that. Philosophy necessarily proceeds by trial and error. We have to find the empirical collective apparatus that allows us to hold together and preserve the diversity of modes, every time – that may well be my contribution, or in any case my pet subject!

NT: So can we say that philosophy is, not the guardian of the temple or temples, but the guardian of the plurality of modes of existence?

BL: Yes. Heidegger says that philosophy is the 'shepherd of Being'. We can re-use that expression because philosophy does indeed have something of the shepherd about it, but in a quite different sense, not in the sense of a leader but in the sense of the one who endeavours to avoid carnage between the wolf and the sheep, and even among the different sheep. That's a much more modest role than that of a metalanguage which would allow us to say what the world is. But it's not a negligible role, either, because it demands that philosophy be constantly attentive to category errors, attentive to the other modes and their tendency to cannibalize each other. Philosophy is a demanding practice, which we musn't forget to see as also being a mode of existence in itself, within this system of modes of existence.

The great philosopher William James put it very well, claiming basically that all philosophy means respecting prepositions. It also means respecting and understanding adverbs: what does 'scientifically' signify? And 'legally' – what does that mean? 'Politically', 'religiously'? If you want to talk scientifically, you have to be able to demonstrate that. If you say you're speaking fictionally, for that to hold water you also have to be able to prove it. If you say 'let's speak technically', it has to fly. If, lastly, you claim to be 'speaking legally', then this so very particular legal bond, which requires so much time to get to, must be able to actually hold up.

NT: I think that expression 'shepherd of Being', read this way, is a very beautiful definition of philosophy.

BL: In a quite different sense from Heidegger's.

NT: The philosopher is shepherd of Being, but not at all the guide who'll take the flock to the right spot!

BL: Philosophy is so beautiful!

NT: Why is it so beautiful for you?

BL: I don't know how to answer that question, except by crying. Philosophy – philosophers know this – is this totally amazing form that's interested in the totality, but that never attains it because the aim is not to attain it, but to love it. Love is philosophy's word.

NT: The love of wisdom.

BL: The love of a wisdom evidently inaccessible ... Basically like the answer to that question. Just joking!

Letter to Lilo

NT: Bruno, what would you say to a person, a citizen, a terrestrial, who would be forty years old when they read this book? You have three grandchildren, including a grandson, Lilo, who is now one. What would you say to Lilo?

BL: What can one say over forty years? I'm not Madame Soleil![1] I'd want to start by telling Lilo that the first twenty years that await him will, I think, be tough. He has every reason to steel himself. I hope he'll study geochemistry or ecology. I don't know.

Given how incredibly slowly we're reacting to the transformation of our past living conditions, partly through the fault of previous generations and my generation in particular, it's clear that habitability isn't going to be produced any time soon. Lilo's generation is going to suffer the consequences of the failures to act of previous years. The result will be that the catastrophes announced by the natural sciences will

---

[1] The late French astrologer, said to have advised François Mitterrand.

fall on him. Obviously, the first piece of advice I'd like to give him is: 'Make sure you seek out all possible therapeutic tools for resisting eco-anxiety over the next twenty years!' We're going to have to equip our children and grandchildren with therapeutic tools for dodging despair.

This is really a difficult exercise you've asked me to do! So I'll allow myself to make a hypothesis that doesn't have the slightest basis: maybe it's better to project ourselves forty years into the future. Because if we look at the succession of generations, the next twenty years will probably be better; we'll doubtless end up coming to grips with the place we find ourselves in, meaning, we'll have landed for good. The number of transformations, of catastrophes, over the past twenty years and those we're living through today will have ended up being assimilable. We will have ended up finding the political institutions, legal definitions, arts, sciences, and probably the transformed economic conditions that will allow us to get by.

It's not the role of a grandfather or a philosopher to herald the end of the world. It will be tough for twenty years, but I think that in the twenty years after that we'll have found a way to resume the civilizing process that was interrupted in the period we're in now. And if we picture me arranging to meet Lilo in forty years' time, at that particular moment we'll look back together, historically, at the period of denial, ignorance, and incomprehension of the ecological situation we got ourselves into, throughout what I call the modern parenthesis. We'll look at it together as an oddity, just as today we look at the Roman

Papist Church of the 13th century, a completely weird kind of form that was very important in its day, that created magnificent things in its time, but which is also completely finished. That's what I hope for the best for Lilo.

Thanks

These interviews owe a lot to preliminary conversations with Veronica Calvo and Bruno Karsenti. Both being close to Bruno Latour and familiar with his work, they followed this book closely right up to its final draft. Rose Vidal revised and edited the text, which allowed it to preserve the spoken nature of the discussion, while constantly meeting the requirement of literarity, with some extracts being published in *Le Monde*, on 11 October 2022. Lastly, Chantal Latour supported this project from its beginnings and helped make sure the dialogue was able to take place in the best possible conditions thanks to her confidence, her steadfastness, and her immense kindness. A very big thanks to all the above, and through them, to all those who made this book possible.

Based on the interview 'Entretien avec Bruno Latour', a film by Nicolas Truong, made by Camille de Chenay and Nicolas Truong (© YAMI 2 /ARTE France – 2021).